Comic Books as History

The Narrative Art of Jack Jackson, Art Spiegelman, and Harvey Pekar

Comic Books as History

Studies in Popular Culture
M. Thomas Inge, General Editor

University Press of Mississippi
Jackson and London

Joseph Witek

The Narrative Art of

Jack Jackson,

Art Spiegelman,

and **Harvey Pekar**

92 91 90   4 3 2

The paper in this book meets the guidelines for perma-
nence and durability of the Committee on Production
Guidelines for Book Longevity of the Council on Library Resources. ∞

Library of Congress Cataloging-in-Publication Data

Witek, Joseph.
    Comic books as history : the narrative art of Jack Jackson,
Art Spiegelman, and Harvey Pekar / Joseph Witek.
        p.   cm. — (Studies in popular culture)
    Bibliography: p.
    Includes index.
    ISBN 0-87805-405-7 (alk. paper). — ISBN 0-87805-406-5
(pbk. : alk. paper)
        1. Comic books, strips, etc.—United States—History and
criticism.   2. United States—Popular culture—History—20th
century.   3. Jackson, Jack, 1941–   .   4. Spiegelman, Art.
5. Pekar, Harvey.   I. Title.   II. Series: Studies in popular
culture (Jackson, Miss.)
PN6725.W58   1989
741.5'0973—dc20   89-16545
                                                          CIP

British Library Cataloguing-in-Publication data available

FOR TERRI

Truth

is stranger and a thousand times

More

Thrilling than

Fiction

—Motto of True Comics

Figures

Preface

A critical and scholarly language for the analysis of comic books has not yet been developed. Those technical terms which do exist generally reflect the ad hoc usage of fan writers and the comic-book creators themselves; I have tried to make terms such as "tier," "splash page," and "breakdowns" as clear and as self-explanatory as possible. The several reference works on comics cited in the bibliography will provide further discussions of the conventions and technical terms used in comics.

Standard scholarly reference forms make no provision for the citation of comic books and related materials; when citing comic books I have included in most cases the issue number, publisher, and printed date of publication. Newcomers to comic books need to be aware that, for arcane reasons having to do with retail stocking practices, comic books are often postdated up to four months after their actual appearance on newsstands and in stores.

Except for the collections of comics by Jack Jackson and Art Spiegelman, few of the comic books discussed here are paginated, and page numbers have for the most part been omitted in citations.

Comic-book artists use a variety of techniques in lettering dialogue to indicate stress and voice tone. In quotations from comic books the main stresses have been indicated as italics; I have not attempted to duplicate the all-capital lettering of most comics balloons. Many artists indicate pauses in dialogue by the use of three or more dots; these pauses have been reproduced here without spaces between the dots to differentiate them from standard ellipses.

This book could never have been written without the inspiration and support of Donald Ault. For their many generous contributions to my work I would also like to thank my editor, Thomas Inge, and my friends, colleagues, and advisors at Vanderbilt University: Vereen Bell, Leonard Folgarait, Phyllis Frus, Roy Gottfried, Michael Kreyling, Cecelia Tichi, and Joe Urgo; I am also grateful to the university for financial support. I am indebted for information on the *Classics Illustrated* comics to Dan Malan, Michael Sawyer, and Charles Heffelfinger, and I am especially grateful for permissions and for many kinds of assistance to the Frawley Corporation, William M. Gaines, Jack Jackson, Harvey Pekar and Joyce Brabner, and Art Spiegelman.

Comic Books as History

The Narrative Art of Jack Jackson, Art Spiegelman, and Harvey Pekar

Introduction

This book presupposes that comic books as narratives and as cultural productions merit serious critical analysis. Recent literary theory has focused attention on the relations between verbal and visual languages; indeed, contemporary semiotics takes as its defining project the reading of images and other nonverbal structures as texts. Though American comic books and comic strips have often been unsophisticated in their subject matter, in form they display a highly developed narrative grammar and vocabulary based on an inextricable combination of verbal and visual elements. More completely than illuminated texts or illustrated novels, Hogarthian picture sequences, or medieval and Renaissance icons, comic books and comic strips integrate words and pictures into a flexible, powerful literary form capable of a wide range of narrative effects. As literary criticism works to develop a visual poetics, an obvious place to start unraveling the relations between word and image is in the complex semiotic process embodied in the comics page of a newspaper or in a comic book from the local newsstand.

A critical analysis of the comic-book form is especially necessary now, when a growing number of contemporary American comic books are being written *as* literature aimed at a general readership of adults and concerned, not with the traditionally escapist themes of comics, but with issues such as the clash of cultures in American history, the burdens of guilt and suffering passed on within families, and the trials and small triumphs of the daily workaday world. The three creators discussed here, Jack Jackson (*Los Tejanos, Comanche Moon*), Art Spiegelman (*Maus: A Survivor's Tale*), and Harvey Pekar (*American Splendor*) have all contributed to a vital body of work in the comic-book form which, in the last fifteen years, has broken away from traditional comic-book formulas while exploiting the rich formal and thematic heritage of the medium.

Art Spiegelman's *Maus*, which was nominated for a National Book Critics Circle Award in biography, recasts the Jewish Holocaust story in terms of cats and mice while it explores the intergenerational tensions between the survivor of a death camp and his writer-artist son; Jack Jackson's revisionist historical tales of the American Southwest attempt to reintroduce the stories of previously excluded figures of American history;[1] in *American Splendor* Harvey Pekar writes what he calls "neo-realist" stories of his own working-class life in Cleveland, and he places himself firmly in the long tradition of American autobiography. The works of all three creators are concerned to varying degrees with the connections between historical and fictional narrative: together they embody a spectrum of historical narrative which ranges from Jackson's overtly politicized rendering of the history of social groups, through world history focused by means of biography and autobiography in Spiegelman's work, to Pekar's history of an individual life.

These three innovators build, each in his own way, on traditional approaches to comics in order to expand the possibilities of the comic-book medium; this is history with a difference. Comic books have taught history lessons before, as does Jack Jackson, but whereas didactic comics generally reinforce a consensus view of American nationalism, Jackson focuses on the stories of the native Americans and of the Texas-Mexicans who were dispossessed and marginalized in American history. Comics are of course the home of the anthropomorphized talking animals, and the Nazis have been stock villains in comics since before World War II, but Art Spiegelman's *Maus* combines the two elements into a historical work which is as bold and shocking in form as it is insightful and eerily effective in execution. Harvey Pekar's influences can be traced to early comic strips, to Borscht Belt comedy, to proletarian and realistic literature, and to the alternative underground comix of the late 1960s, but *American Splendor* recounts the life and times of a single individual as no comic book has done before.

By basing their comic books on factual occurrences and on personal experiences, all three creators explore the road not taken by most American comic books, which have usually, though not always, eschewed history in favor of fantasy, adventure, and horror. The present discussion of Jackson, Spiegelman, and Pekar arises in part from an attempt to show how the long buried tradition of historical stories, fact-based educational narratives, and committed political expression in comic-book form has finally resulted in the 1980s in the meticulous historical detail of *Comanche Moon* and *Los Tejanos*, the psychologically astute genre mixing of *Maus*, and the relentless autobiographical candor of *American Splendor*.

The thematic and narrative maturity that all these works display helps account in part for an unprecedented cultural interest in comic books; the nomination of *Maus* for the National Book Critics Circle Award is but one example of the wide media attention comic books have received in the late 1980s. In addition, the traditionally cheap and flimsy reproduction of commercial comic books is increasingly giving way to upgraded physical formats; the work of all three of these creators has been collected in trade paperback form and can be found on bookstore shelves rather than in the newsstand haunts of most previous comic books.

It is clear that the comic book, a widely accessible and commercially available medium, is now being chosen as a form by serious writers whose themes have traditionally been expressed in the forms of verbal narratives (both literary and historiographical) and in films and other visual narratives, such as the photo essay. And the change in comic-book marketing strategies has a corollary; a general reading audience now exists in the United States for narratives written in a medium which has historically been considered solely the domain of subliterate adolescent fantasies and of the crassest commercial exploitation of rote generic formulas. Comic art is thus a literary medium in transition from mass popularity and cultural disdain to a new respectability as a means of expression and communication, and this new respect is evident first in the attitudes of the creators themselves. Whether the comic-book form will make good its bid for wider cultural acceptance as adult literature remains to be seen, but it is worth remembering that the major modes of artistic expression of this century, the novel and the cinema, were both at first scorned as vulgarities until serious artists demonstrated their potential.

One index of the shift in cultural attitudes about this "crossbreeding of illustration and prose" is the appearance of a new term for the medium: "sequential art." Both the quotation and the term come from Will Eisner's *Comics and Sequential Art*, the first fulllength discussion of "the unique aesthetics of Sequential Art as a means of creative expression, a distinct discipline, an art and literary form."[2] While the term is not yet in widespread use, "sequential art" has the advantage of avoiding the generic connotations of the word "comic" and sidestepping associations with the burlesque and the ridiculous.

Eisner uses "sequential art" to denote the overall mode of narrative of which both comic strips and comic books are specific and distinct forms. The conceptual limits of the term are still undefined, but a prerequisite for inclusion in the category is a mixture of words (at least potentially) and pictures; wordless visual narratives such as Trajan's column and medieval pictorial tapestries do not qualify, while William Blake's engraved texts and the picture series of Hogarth and Thomas Rowlandson certainly do. "Sequential art" may attain general currency as past pretenders such as "pictorial fiction" did not, but having an overall name for the entire medium not only helps discriminate among kinds of pictorial narratives but also makes possible a finer distinction between the two most common forms of sequential art expression in our culture: comic strips and comic books. These two forms are usually subsumed under the rubric of "the comics," which obscures the important differences between them.

The difference between comic strips and comic books seems at first to be one simply of length: a comic strip is a brief series of panels, a comic book a longer one. Indeed, comic books began life in the 1930s as anthologies of reprinted newspaper comic strips. But comic books have evolved their own generic, narrative, and formal conventions; they are not simply bloated comic strips. While comic strips and comic books are both manifestations of the sequential art medium and both share a common narrative vocabulary and grammar, they diverge so fundamentally as to constitute different literary forms. They differ in their situations in the marketplace, in their cultural status, in their physical mode of presentation, and in the reading conventions they evoke.

Comic strips come to us unbidden, as supplementary features of a daily or Sunday newspaper, and their gratuitous nature imposes on them formal and thematic constraints: comic strips must be brief enough to fit the space requirements of copy editors, and their themes must be general (and genteel) enough to appeal to a broad audience. As a result, most comic strips which survive today are "gag" strips, usually three or four panels (or twice that on Sunday) ending each day with a humorous punch line. Even the continuity strips (those with an ongoing story line), such as *Mary Worth* or *Judge Parker*, are paced slowly enough and are narratively redundant enough to accommodate the reader who looks in on the plot only occasionally. Comic books, on the other hand, are voluntary purchases, and their themes are tailored to specific audiences. For example, the major comic-book publishers have offered commercially viable books (that is, books having a circulation of six figures) ranging from the juvenile television spin-off *Care Bears* to the apocalyptically violent political satire *Elektra: Assassin*.[3] The former is too puerile, the latter too outré to fit newspaper demographics, but both books have had a cadre of loyal readers who make the trip to the local newsstand or comics specialty shop to get them.

Since comic strips are one entertainment feature among many in the newspaper, no particular social stigma is attached to adults who read them; bankers and lawyers can exchange views on the latest *Beetle Bailey* or *Hagar the Horrible* without being considered irretrievable vulgarians. In fact, some classic strips, such as George Herriman's celebrated *Krazy Kat*, appealed primarily to a grown-up audience that included such eminences as Pablo Picasso, Charlie Chaplin, and both Edmund Wilson and Woodrow Wilson. The first exhibition of comic art held at a major American museum, "Seventy-five Years of the Comics" at the New York Cultural Center in 1971, consisted almost entirely of comic strips.[4] Conversely, the periodic conservative purges against the supposedly pernicious moral and psychological effects of comics are directed for the most part at comic books, which have been blamed for offenses ranging from teenage eyeball mutilation to illiteracy (though comic books have been used successfully in adult literacy programs).

Comic books have suffered as an artistic form from this virulent cultural hostility; the reactionary restrictions of the comic-book industry's self-censoring body, the Comics Code Authority, led to the thematic stagnation of the sequential art medium for several decades. But though the anti-comic-book crusaders often border on hysteria in the charges they make against comic books, in a sense they are right: comic books in America tap into an imaginative vein which runs closer to primal fears and desires than do newspaper comic strips. Even under the constraints of the Comics Code, the power fantasies embodied in Superman and Batman do finally threaten the comfortable bourgeois worldview exemplified by Dagwood Bumstead and Charlie Brown.

Comic strips have not always dealt primarily in domestic comedy and soap-opera melodrama. In fact, the comic strip form has produced some of its greatest achievements in other styles and genres, such as the stunning visual displays of Winsor McCay's *Little Nemo in Slumberland* and Lyonel Feininger's *Wee Willie Winkie's World*; the complex episodic adventures of E. C. Segar's *Popeye* (*Thimble Theater*) and Floyd Gottfredson's *Mickey Mouse*; and the sweeping transhistorical romances of Harold Foster's *Prince Valiant* and Alex Raymond's *Flash Gordon*. But these comic strips are the past, as moribund today as epic poetry. Since at least the end of the 1950s, the potential in the sequential art medium for visual impact and narrative drive has been increasingly displaced from strips onto comic books. The most obvious reason for the formal shift is the growing technical restrictions to which newspaper strips have been subjected.

The major newspaper syndicates (which distribute the daily and Sunday strips) have severely reduced the standard size of comic strips several times in recent years, and layout editors often require that strip artists supply "throwaway" panels, which can be printed or deleted as space requires. Meticulous visual detail and closely plotted action thus of necessity gives way to broadly caricatured figures and primarily verbal humor. Comic books, however, have become ever more technically sophisticated: panel shapes and sizes are usually limited only by the artist's imagination, better printing techniques have improved four-color separation, and paper of higher quality (including partially coated stock) is currently supplanting cheap newsprint in much comic book production. This last change largely reflects the demands of comic book hobbyists, who in the past could only watch in horror as their expensive collections of comic books printed on highly acid paper disintegrated over time into worthless wood pulp.

But the physical differences between comic strips and comic books are much more fundamental than variations in printing quality; their differing attributes as physical artifacts require differing structures of thought in reading them. As a formal unit the comic strip is short, meant to be read in seconds or a few minutes at most in daily installments, and from this compression comes the comic strip's power to surprise and to please. Even the continuity strips, with their ostensible narrative basis, depend for their effects on accretion of incidents and repetition of motifs rather than on a building causal sequence of events; a *Steve Canyon* adventure typically ends not with a dramatic climax but with a falling away of characters as the ageless hero drifts into another conflict. Only rarely does the first panel of a comic strip depend upon the last panel of the previous day's sequence; more often the strip simply repeats the needed information, which accounts for the two-steps-back-one-step-forward rhythm of the continuity strips.

Comic books work in much larger and longer segments; the page, two-page spreads, multipage stories, and book-length and multi-book-length stories are the structural units of comic-book narratives. The increased length of comic books provides wide opportunities for detailed exposition, complex visual/verbal effects, pacing in time and space, and what Will Eisner calls "reader discipline,"[5] artistic control of how a reader perceives a narrative structure. Comic books can be discursive and oblique in their narrative and thematic connections; comic strips are of necessity concentrated, with each verbal and visual element directed to a single and immediate effect: the termination of a strip becomes its rationale. A strip's unity is perceived visually, with its closure present to the reader's sight. Comic books, like all long printed narratives, promise but continually defer their endings until the final page.

One comic strip which does not deliver the promised closure helps to prove the rule: Herriman's *Krazy Kat* generates energy in its narrative by continually giving plausible but ultimately inadequate rationales which purport to explain the strip's surreal action but do not; instead they thwart and mock the reader's expectations for closure by supplying an illusory teleology. Comic strips and comic books finally demand that their readers bring to them differing sets of expectations about the methods, design, and probable effect of each of the two forms of sequential art.

This formal distinction, crucial as it is to the practical reading of sequential art narratives, has rarely been articulated or even acknowledged in either general or academic discussions of the medium. Until relatively recently most writers on comics, in the words of one comics historian, "either [have] avoided the comic book completely or have treated it as a minor offshoot of the comic strip."[6] For example, the only comprehensive reference work in the comics field, Maurice Horn's massive *World Encyclopedia of Comics*, treats comic books as a variant format of the (implicitly normative) comic strip, and most other full-length studies likewise deal solely or primarily with comic strips.[7] The only extended discussions in print about comic books before the 1960s were sociological studies by Gershon Legman, Fredric Wertham, and Geoffrey Wagner.[8] All were uniformly negative in their assessments of comic books: "Legman, Wertham, and Wagner compete in their merciless castigation of the comics, heaping blazing coals upon them for their excesses of violence and gore, their often unwholesome treatment of sex, and their frequently low level of writing and drawing."[9] When sympathetic discussions of comic books did appear in the United States, they were generally more nostalgic than analytical; the main exception is Les Daniels's survey *Comix: A History of Comic Books in America.*[10] The rise of semiotic studies and an accompanying interest in the relations of verbal and visual languages has spawned several academic analyses of comic books, while an increased general interest in individual comic-book artists has focused attention on some of the long-time masters of the form.[11]

But there has been as yet little formal critical response to a growing body of work in the comic-book form which presents itself with no apologies as adult literature while at the same time maintaining its links to established comic-book genres and themes. The works of Harvey Pekar, Art Spiegelman, and Jack Jackson, while they owe and acknowledge their debts to the great comic-book craftsmen of the past, confront issues such as the relations of historical and fictional discourse and the connections between ideology and narrative on a scale unprecedented in the history of sequential art.

American Splendor, Maus, and *Comanche Moon* and *Los Tejanos* offer unique opportunities for a narrative analysis of the medium, not because they are better in kind than *Batman* or *Uncle Scrooge,* but because their literary and historical emphases allow access to established lines of critical thought in literature and historiography while they eliminate as variables some of the intriguing but distracting thematic peculiarities of traditional commercial comics: their stylized and inconsequential violence, their deflection of sexuality into sadomasochism and male bonding, their obsession with costumed power figures.[12] Many American comic books indeed pander to juvenile tastes, but despite the amazement of most recent media commentators at the idea of serious literature in comic-book form, comics such as *Maus* and *American Splendor* did not arise ex nihilo or as the high-culture spawn of Roy Lichtenstein; they are the most recent and most culturally visible manifestations of a minor but long-established tradition of historical and fact-based comic-book narratives.

The surprise is not that serious stories can be told in comic-book form but that such work took so long to attract the attention of the general culture. Spiegelman's *Maus* would not exist were it not for the superb comic books of Carl Barks and Walt Kelly, as well as for the twists given to the funny-animal genre in the underground comix of the 1960s and 1970s;[13] Jack Jackson's history comics take the conventions of western and horror comics and lay bare their political and social implications; Pekar's autobiographical stories exploit a whole spectrum of sequential art modes ranging from the vaudevillelike blackouts of early comic strips to the political passion of the undergrounds.

The emergence of comic books as a respectable literary form in the 1980s *is* unlooked for, given the long decades of cultural scorn and active social repression, but the potential has always existed for comic books to present the same kinds of narratives as other verbal and pictorial media. One way to begin to understand the seemingly sudden appearance of comic-book histories and autobiographies aimed at an adult audience is to consider the heritage of fact-based comic books in America and then to ask how such comic books function as narrative media and as embodiments of ideology. Art Spiegelman has said: "One of the things that was important to me in *Maus* was to make it all true."[14] This claim to literal truth distinguishes the works of Jackson, Spiegelman, and Pekar from most previous comic books. The present analysis of the sequential art medium therefore begins with a consideration of some other comic books which have made that claim of truth before.

1. Jack Jackson often writes under the pen name of "Jaxon."
2. Will Eisner, *Comics and Sequential Art* (Tamarac, Fla.: Poorhouse Press, 1985), 5.
3. Commercial comic-book publishing is dominated by Marvel Comics and DC Comics (formerly known as National Periodical Publications).
4. Maurice Horn, *The World Encyclopedia of Comics* (New York: Chelsea House, 1976), 46. An exhibition titled "The Comic Strip: Its History and Significance" was held at the American Institute of Graphic Arts in 1942, before comic books were well established as a separate narrative form; see Rheinhold Reitberger and Wolfgang Fuchs, *Comics: Anatomy of a Mass Medium* (Boston: Little, Brown, 1972), 11.
5. Eisner, *Sequential Art*, 19.
6. Dick Lupoff and Don Thompson, *All in Color for a Dime* (New Rochelle, N.Y.: Arlington House, 1970), 8 (introduction).
7. For example, see Martin Sheridan, *The Comics and Their Creators* (1942); Coulton Waugh, *The Comics* (1947); Stephen Becker, *Comic Art in America* (1959); Alan Aldridge and George Perry, *Penguin Book of Comics* (1967); and Jerry Robinson, *The Comics: An Illustrated History of Comic Strip Art* (1974). My bibliography provides full publishing information.
8. Gershon Legman, *Love and Death: A Study in Censorship* (New York: Breaking Point, 1949); Fredric Wertham, *Seduction of the Innocent* (New York: Rinehart and Winston, 1954); Geoffrey Wagner, "Popular Iconography in the U.S.A.," in *Parade of Pleasure* (New York: Library Publishers, 1955).

9. Lupoff and Thompson, *All in Color,* 9.

10. Les Daniels, *Comix: A History of Comic Books in America* (New York: Bonanza Books, 1971). Other books about comic books include Jules Feiffer, *The Great Comic Book Heroes* (1965); Lupoff and Thompson, *All in Color* and *The Comic-Book Book* (1971); Michael Barrier and Martin Williams, eds., *A Smithsonian Book of Comic-Book Comics* (1981); and Ron Goulart, *Great History of Comic Books* (1986). My bibliography provides full publishing information.

11. For example, the monumental thirty-volume *Carl Barks Library of Walt Disney's Donald Duck* (Scottsdale, Ariz.: Another Rainbow, 1983–) contains a series of literary analyses of Barks's work; Will Eisner's *Comics and Sequential Art* is an important critical contribution by one of the central figures of comic-book history.

12. Such issues deserve and have received study, as in, for example, Erling B. Holtsmark, "*Magnus Robot-Fighter:* The Future Looks at the Present through the Past," *Journal of Popular Culture* 12 (1979): 702–720.

13. For the origin and usage of the term "comix" for alternative comic books produced by independent publishers, see "Comix, Not Comics," in Jay Kennedy, ed., *The Official Underground and Newave Comix Price Guide* (Cambridge, Mass.: Harmony Books, 1982), 11.

14. Art Spiegelman, interview on "Fresh Air," National Public Radio, WPLN, Nashville, December 1986.

Comic Books as History: The First Shot at Fort Sumter

Comic books in America have not often been used to tell stories about real lives and actual events. The comics tradition for us lies elsewhere: in the realms of fantasy, of wish fulfillment, of projections of power, and in the ritual repetition of generic formulas. Their landscape is typically the skyscraper canyons of Superman's Metropolis, the dank back alleys of Batman's Gotham City, the standardized suburbia of Archie's Riverdale High, or the glittering cash mountains of Uncle Scrooge's money bins. Even those physical and temporal spaces in the comics which most resemble our own in specific detail become in fact the mindscapes of our cultural imagination. The Phantom's deepest Africa, the wild West of Zorro and the Lone Ranger, the World War II of the flying Blackhawks, and, in the newspaper comic strips, the Middle Ages of Prince Valiant and the Great Depression of Little Orphan Annie: all these times and places serve mainly as colorful historical backdrops for their manifestly fictional protagonists.

Before the last two decades, the exceptions to the general rule of comic-book fantasy fell almost entirely into marginal genres of the already culturally marginal comic-book medium. Comics which attempted to tell true (or ostensibly true) stories were usually either didactic efforts to edify the adolescents or sensational real-life analogues to the comic-book industry's pulpy stock-in-trades. The "preachies" included biblical retellings, such as *Bible Stories for Young Folk*; inspirational biographies, such as the Democratic National Committee's 1948 giveaway *The Story of Harry S. Truman*, the Catechetical Guild's *Pius XII: Man of Peace,* and the 1952 *Thrilling True Story of the Baseball Giants;* or else they were of the educational "how things work" genre of industrial and corporate giveaways, such as the Federal Reserve Bank of New York's *The Story of Checks.*[1]

Much more popular than the rather dry informational comics were the "real-life adventures" comic books. These comics mined history and historical legends in order to feed the voracious comic-book genre markets, including Westerns (*Davy Crockett, True Story of Jesse James, Custer's Last Fight*); crime and gangsters (*True Crime Comics*); horror and the supernatural (several comic-book versions of the venerable *Ripley's Believe It or Not!* series); and adventure (*True Aviation Picture Stories, It Really Happened*). Combining both the informational and sensational impulses in a single anthology was the wholesome *True Comics,* which ran from 1941 to 1950 and featured sports and popular biographies, patriotic history, and true FBI adventures, all published by Parents Magazine Press.

But the premier American producer of comic books that were good for you was the Gilberton Company, which for almost thirty years published the redoubtable *Classics Comics* and *Classics Illustrated* series. While the company was best known for comic-book redactions of literary works and popular stories, Gilberton also issued semiannual *Classics Illustrated Special Issues* and a monthly educational series called *The World Around Us.* Unlike more dubious claimants to literal veracity on the newsstands, such as *True Love Confessions,* the Gilberton fact-based comics were impeccably researched and handsomely produced. In fact, some artwork from Gilberton comics was eventually used to illustrate school textbooks, an unheard-of height of respectability for comic-book art at the time.[2]

The Gilberton comics, which exemplify the didactic strain of comic books, were popular in the 1950s with parents, who were willing to buy, say, *The Story of the Coast Guard* for their children at a time when the kids themselves could buy on the newsstands comic books which presented the lurid and antisocial elements of comic-book fantasies with an unprecedented graphic power. Diametrically opposed to the wholesome literary and social aspirations of the Gilberton comics were the stupendously gruesome excesses of publisher William M. Gaines's E.C. Comics. Such titles as *The Vault of Horror, Tales from the Crypt, Weird Science, Shock SuspenStories,* and *The Haunt of Fear* became legendary and notorious for their beautifully crafted and gleefully perverse transgressions of almost every imaginable cultural taboo, including thematic treatments of incest, bondage and sadomasochism, dismemberment and disembowelment, and family murders of every possible combination. Cannibalism and necrophilia were so ubiquitous in the E.C. comics as to constitute the leitmotif of the E.C. house style. These E.C. "New Trend" comics and their more slovenly imitators helped focus social and governmental antagonism toward comic books in general; a congressional investigation and the threat of federal anticomic legislation sparked the creation in 1954 of the comic-book industry's self-regulating Comics Code Authority, in its words the "most stringent code in existence for any communications media."[3] Sucked bloodless by the censors, the E.C. comics quickly died, leaving behind only the magazine-sized parody comic *Mad*, purveyor of ironic skepticism and adolescent iconoclasm since 1952. The short-lived E.C. revolution also bequeathed to American kids a latent heritage in comic books of rebellion against the dominant culture which would come to fruition fifteen years later in the underground comix.

Ironically enough, the letters "E.C.," which came to mean "Entertaining Comics," originally stood for "Educational Comics," the rubric under which William Gaines's father, M. C. Gaines, founded the company and published in the mid-1940s the various *Picture Stories* series, including comics on the Bible, American history, world history, and science. The elder Gaines failed in his efforts to market his didactic comic books directly to elementary schools. After his father's death in 1947, William Gaines took over the nearly moribund E.C. Publications and presided over the subsequent explosion of horror, science fiction, crime, and war comics in the 1950s. But in this last genre—war comics—the original E.C. didactic impulse lived on. Under editor Harvey Kurtzman, both of E.C.'s war titles, *Frontline Combat* and *Two-Fisted Tales*, often featured stories based on historical fact, and even the fictional war stories were painstakingly researched and rich in accurate period detail. Sensational they are, with graphic depictions of the process of organized death beyond the wildest nightmares of the staid Gilberton Company. But in the best of their factual pieces, such as the series on the American Civil War, the E.C. comics are as committed to historical veracity as both their highbrow rival *Classics Illustrated* and the most serious of academic historians.[4]

A comparison of the narrative treatments of the same historical event, the first shot at Fort Sumter, as depicted in a *Classics Illus-*

trated Special Issue, in E.C.'s *Frontline Combat,* and in Shelby Foote's prose account in his popular history *The Civil War: A Narrative* provides a framework for a consideration of the narrative strategies of the comic-book medium and also allows for a contrast of the interpretive procedures necessary for an analysis of prose and sequential art narratives.

Shelby Foote's Fort Sumter

The subject of these three narratives is a powerful one: the mythical beginning of America's most intense cultural trauma, the Civil War. To call it mythical is not to say that it is false but instead to stress that the perceived significance of the moment is the outcome of a narrative choice, that as a culture we have determined that the story we call "the Civil War" begins with a cannon shot fired in Charleston Harbor, South Carolina, on 12 April 1861. It matters not a whit to our historical imaginations that politically motivated sectional bloodshed had occurred regularly throughout the previous decade, that firearms had been discharged incidental to the transfer of power from the Federal government to the seceded states, or even that, on 9 January 1861, in Charleston Harbor, Confederate cannons had fired on a United States ship bearing supplies for the Fort Sumter garrison. The watershed event has become this early-morning mortar shot and none other, and no historical research or fortuitous documentary discovery can change its status as an epochal event.

The point here is that a formal comparison of historical texts must take into account a complex set of prior narrative choices which establish the field and boundaries of each particular telling of events. "Fort Sumter" has become shorthand for the beginning of a crucial historical phase, but to explain it as a beginning requires some understanding of its ending: the meaning ascribed to the events of 12 April 1861, thus depends on how one reads the entire process supposedly inaugurated on that date. Which of the several competing stories of the Civil War are we being told (and are we prepared to read)? Each account of Fort Sumter must contend with and mediate among assumptions generated in the culture by the various stories told as "the Civil War": the ultimate reconciliation of quarreling brothers under the United States Constitution; the tragic apocalypse of a Southern chivalric culture; the inevitable eradication of a quasi-feudal economic system; the long-deferred manumission of the oppressed black race, or one of many variations and syntheses of such stories.

The three present examples purport to depict the same historical moment, so they naturally share significant elements.[5] Despite the difference in narrative media, Foote's prose account and the *Classics Illustrated* version resemble each other more closely in several important respects than do the two comic-book treatments. Both Foote and the *Classics* comic cover the same time span (from shortly after midnight to dawn on April 12, 1861), mention and depict the same principals (the Confederate envoys, Major Robert Anderson, General Beauregard), and present some of the same particulars, such as the crowds of spectators watching from the Charleston rooftops. The opening page of the E.C. story, "First Shot," concentrates on the actual shot itself and hence depicts in five panels what the *Classics* comic shows in one panel and Foote's text treats in a single sentence. All three accounts agree on the time of the shot, 4:30 A.M., and each uses the climactic verb "burst."

But the versions vary widely in point of view, in tone, and in the ideological implications each draws from the events it represents. This is not to say that one or the other is more historically precise, though some discrepancies among the accounts do occur. Rather it is to focus on the varying ways these narratives deploy the conventions of each medium to make truth claims about an event that is "already told," already so weighted with cultural significance that any telling risks the loss of its individual rhetorical force in the face of previously established readings and individual associations. Each teller must hew closely enough to the "known" story to seem factually accurate while at the same time presenting a narrative emotionally compelling enough to be worth the retelling.[6]

To achieve these contrasting goals, Foote's narrative both exploits and subverts the linearity of chronological prose narration. The account foregrounds the traditional empirical indexes of scientific historiography: times, dates, and numbers, implying that the historical past is seamlessly connected to our present through chronology and numerical sequence:

> It was now past midnight, the morning of April 12; there could be no delay, for advance units of the relief expedition had been sighted off the bar. This time four men went out in the white-flagged boat, empowered by Beauregard to make the decision without further conferences, according to Anderson's answer. He heard their demand and replied that he

would evacuate the fort "by noon of the 15th instant" unless he received "controlling instructions from my government, or additional supplies." This last, of course, with the relief fleet standing just outside the harbor—though Anderson did not know it had arrived—made the guarantee short-lived at best and therefore unacceptable to the aides, who announced that Beauregard would open fire "in one hour from this time." It was then 3.20 a.m. Anderson, about to test his former gunnery student in a manner neither had foreseen in the West Point classroom, shook the hands of the four men and told them in parting: "If we do not meet again in this world, I hope we may meet in the better one." Without returning to Beauregard's headquarters, they proceeded at once to Cummings Point and gave the order to open fire.

One of the four was Roger Pryor, the Virginian who had spoken from a Charleston balcony just two days ago. "Strike a blow!" he had urged the Carolinians. Now when he was offered the honor of firing the first shot, he shook his head, his long hair swaying. "I could not fire the first gun of the war," he said, his voice as husky with emotion as Anderson's had been, back on the wharf at the fort. Another Virginian could and would— white-haired Edmund Ruffin, a farm-paper editor and old-line secessionist, sixty-seven years of age. At 4.30 he pulled a lanyard; the first shot of the war drew a parabola against the sky and burst with a glare, outlining the dark pentagon of Fort Sumter.

Friday dawned crimson on the water as the siege got under way. Beauregard's forty-seven howitzers and mortars began a bombardment which the citizens of Charleston, together with people who had come from miles around by train and buggy, on horseback and afoot to see the show, watched from the rooftops as from grandstand seats at a fireworks display, cheering as the gunnery grew less ragged and more accurate, until at last almost every shot was jarring the fort itself.[7]

For all its clarity and smooth prose, this passage is, as any historical narration must be, highly manipulative rhetoric. Supporting the "objective" dates and numbers is a complex web of verb tenses and time shifts which determine the point of view of the passage and focus our interpretation of its central action. This account is, in fact, largely from the perspective of the Confederate government; its syntax and grammar stress the immediacy of the situation and the urgency of the need to open fire, even though it is clearly not the case for the Union side that "there could be no delay," as Major Anderson's temporizing reply makes clear. Myriad temporal indicators like "was now," "this time," "at once," "was then," and "now" anchor the account in a narrative present, while shifting verb tenses help to relate the immediate action to a series of implicitly significant past events: a previous conference between Anderson and Beauregard's aides, the sighting of the relief expedition, the West Point connection between the commanders, and Roger Pryor's speech in Charleston. Foote thus attempts to satisfy his audience's expectations for accurate historical data and for a coherent and gripping explanation of the events.

Foote explicates a process of history in which individual character and action is at least as important as contingent circumstance or more impersonal workings of power. Beneath the overt confrontation between rival political entities lies another tension, one that cuts across the sectional battle lines: the conflict between people who are weak and ambivalent and those who are strong and certain about the war to come. Major Anderson's stand in the middle of Charleston Harbor is shown to be an act not of defiance but of powerlessness; without "controlling instructions from [his] government," he can do nothing. His opposite number, General Beauregard, who now outranks his former teacher, has potency to spare, since he can "empower" the nameless "four men" to act in his stead, and he himself will "open fire" if their demands are not met. Anderson's parting sentiments suggest a fatalistic, indeed melodramatic, resignation to the coming events; he is genial toward the men who will soon attack him, and his thoughts are on his eternal reward rather than on the military struggle about to ensue.

The monolithic depiction of the Confederate embassy breaks to reveal that one of the men is Anderson's emotional counterpart, a connection made explicitly by the text. Roger Pryor, erstwhile fire-eating rabble-rouser, cannot bring himself to perform the symbolic act he advocated so fiercely; his once strong voice is now "husky with emotion as Anderson's had been." In contrast is the patriarchal "white-haired Edmund Ruffin," who takes and is given responsibility for firing "the first shot of the war." This account insists repeatedly on the significance of the shot itself. The careful recounting of the final moments before it occurs, Pryor's dramatic last-minute reluctance, and the repetitions of the phrase "first shot" combine to reinforce the traditional meanings invested in the event. The Civil War started here, the narrative says, and Edmund Ruffin started it. History is in this account the outcome of personal human choices; had Ruffin too declined to initiate the originating event, this passage suggests, the entire destructive process of the war might have been averted or altered, so that the causal chain of history need not lead inevitably (for better or worse) to our own present.

When the prose account attempts to incorporate visual or descriptive details for dramatic effect, the inescapable linearity of words in a sentence requires that the relative significance of each particular image can be indicated only by syntactical subordination. Thus, the white flag and Ruffin's white hair, his sixty-seven years and Beauregard's forty-seven guns, and the red of the shot's parabola and the crimson of the dawn are imagistically and grammatically equivalent, and while readers of military history know that the number of cannons in a siege takes precedence over the age of the cannoneers, the text itself cannot make that point directly.

Comics as History Textbooks

In the presentation of their images, comics inevitably differ significantly from prose, and the pages from the *Classics Illustrated* story demonstrate how sequential art narratives establish a visual text parallel to the verbal one, a narration both immediate and subliminal, one which can reinforce, contrast, or even contradict the verbal level of the story. As these two pages are actually the recto and verso of a single leaf, they are a bit misleading as a sequence. The largest perceptual unit of comic-book storytelling is the two-page spread, since, once past the first inside page, or "splash" page, readers are at least peripherally aware of the configurations of both pages which are open before them.[8] The single-page layout is also an important narrative element; in figure 1, the artist, the eminent comic-book creator Jack Kirby, uses four panels in two tiers per page, sometimes called a "two-deep" layout. The panels are identical in size and shape, so that each panel bears a similar narrative emphasis and visual weight. In this case the layout supports, indeed is the first indication of, an overall feeling of solidity and methodical movement. As the figures within the panels are firmly grounded against the panel borders, the panels themselves are buttressed by their identically configured neighbors, much like the flagstones and bricks which represent Fort Sumter's interior. But lest we overstate the thematic influence of panel layout per se, it should be noted that Kirby often uses this same two-deep layout for sequences of the most kinetic superhero action; there the regularity of the panels arguably makes the narrative more chaotic rather than more coherent.[9] What determines this difference is the artistic process called "break-

Figure 1. Jack Kirby, "April, 1861: Fort Sumter," page 2
© The Frawley Corporation

The First Shot at Fort Sumter   **21**

downs," the blocking out of the visual perspective and time of action for each panel.

An individual comic-book panel conventionally depicts an emblematic moment in time from a representative point in space; one of the principal skills of comic-book narration lies in selecting from among the nearly infinite potential choices the most effective points and moments to match the thematic movement of the story. Much of the action of a comic-book story takes place *between* the panels, in the gutters, so to speak, which separate the panels. The pace of the narrative flow depends upon the difficulty of the transitions we are asked, or rather forced, to make, on the amount of bridging material we as readers must supply in moving from panel to panel. Here "April, 1861: Fort Sumter" makes relatively short and logical moves in time and space between panels, while superhero and fantasy comics often use bizarre temporal jumps and irrational perspectives. The panel layouts and the compositional breakdowns thus work together to create a movement at once pictorial and literary; this reading movement is the unique rhythm of the medium of sequential art.

One of our clearest guides to the connections we must make between panels comes in the form of verbal text, and the spaces within the panels which contain that text are themselves "readable" elements. The conventional signs which indicate the status of verbal text in comics are well known: words in oblong boxes function as a narrative voice, words in rounded "balloons" with pointed projections represent direct speech, cloudlike balloons with circles leading to a human figure indicate unspoken thoughts, shaded and capitalized letters denote various degrees of emotion and emphasis, and so forth.[10] The several ways the *Classics Illustrated* story varies from comic-book typographical norms help illuminate the visual function and thematic implications of these textual spaces.

Each panel is headed by a boxed segment of verbal text. Some of the information is crucial to the story: the times, dates, and names so prominent in Shelby Foote's account. Some supplements the visual action: "One of the Confederate officers shook his head." Some is partially redundant: "Two hours later, Anderson gave his answer" above a picture of Anderson giving his answer. But the unvarying placement of these boxes of text suggests that the visual information is subordinate to the verbal, that the pictures are visual glosses on the words above them. The unusual shape of the dialogue balloons also privileges the verbal elements even more than is usual in comics. Balloons always set speech apart from other elements in a comic-book panel, of course, but instead of the conventional round white blobs that really do look something like balloons, here we have speech enclosed in elongated ruled boxes with only rounded corners to indicate semiotically the "balloonness" of the shapes.

The enlarged initial letter of each narrative caption recalls the chapter headings of the King James Bible and lends a note of near-ponderous solemnity to the narrative voice. But the most obvious typographical effect on these pages is, of course, the mechanical-looking lettering. A hallmark of the Gilberton comics, this stenciled lettering has rarely been used by other major comic-book publishers except for E.C. Publications, which stenciled the captions and balloons in its text-heavy horror and science fiction titles (but not in the war titles).[11]

With these notable exceptions, dialogue balloons and caption boxes in comic books are almost always hand lettered for two reasons, one practical and one aesthetic. It is much easier with hand lettering to make the required speech fit exactly into the available space in the panels; here the blank spaces in the balloons on both lower panels of the first page show that type can lead to wasted space. More immediately to the point for a formal analysis of comic books, freehand lettering, no matter how precisely done, always betrays the calligrapher's hand, and thus more closely approximates the nuances of the human voice than does mechanically produced type. But what the *Classics Illustrated* comic gives up in expressive range it gains in at least the cachet of respectability and at best what Will Eisner calls "a kind of inherent authority" as a result of the impersonality of "cold type."[12]

The cumulative effects of these devices (the physically superior placement of the verbal elements, the ruled dialogue balloons, the enlarged initial letters of the captions, the mechanical letters) are to establish a tone of stateliness and legitimized power and incidentally to emphasize the importance of words over pictures. This logocentricity is implicit in the basic premise of the Gilberton Company, a publishing house which was founded as a means of introducing the canonical texts of Western culture to a generation increasingly in the thrall of nonprint media. The authoritative tone too is very much a part of the Gilberton Company's entire didactic project, but here it also reinforces important themes expressed in the visual subtext of the Fort Sumter story.

The layout of the pages and the composition of the individual panels, especially in the configurations of the human figures, combine to create a world that is solidly grounded in space, with clear and logical power relationships among the people in it. Moreover, the visual perspectives in the panels ensure that the audience is likewise firmly placed vis-à-vis the action, and this grounding has a clear political consequence. In contrast to the southern perspective of Foote's account, our point of view here is subtly but inescapably from the Union side. While the verbal text presents much of the same information as does the passage from Foote, the pictorial elements belie Foote's implication of Anderson's (and the fort's) weakness. Panel by panel the combined words and pictures in this narrative suggest that Fort Sumter, its garrison, and by extension the political order that both represent are not vitally threatened by the impending Confederate attack.

The perspective in the first panel places us inside Fort Sumter in the position of the corporal of the guard being addressed. The two Union sentries dominate the foreground and middle ground, while the oncoming boat (perhaps filled with enemies) in the background is dwarfed by the massive stones of the wharf. The first sentry's rifle physically blocks the entrance up to the fort, and his wide stance suggests that he will not be easily moved. His speech might seem doubly redundant, since it repeats information given in both the caption and in the visual text, but it serves the crucial thematic function of invoking the military chain of command, just as the head-on perspective implicates the audience in that paradigm of properly subordinated authority. The sequence of ranks allows the action between the first and second panels to be dropped out, since military etiquette allows us to assume that the envoys have been greeted, vetted, and introduced to Anderson, along with all the other necessary but irrelevant physical details required to get them from their boat in the water to their seats around the commander's conference table.

The pictorial composition of the second panel suggests an at least provisional balance of power between the antagonists-to-be. The three Confederate officers (not the four of Foote's version) slightly overbalance Anderson at the table, but they in turn are commanded by the Union guards in the background; the sergeant looming on the left has his hand ready on his pistol holster. Anderson's speech balloon visually caps the scene, establishing his control of the action. The potentially dominant head of the Confederate officer in the right foreground is physically disrupted by his colleague's right arm and compositionally balanced by the lampshade to the left. At first glance Anderson might seem to be reading his words from the paper before him, but his repeated use of first-person pronouns focuses the verbal text on the Union commander and his power of possession ("mine," "my") rather than on the rebel demands for his surrender.

Anderson's comment in this panel about knowing Beauregard demonstrates a potential weakness of sequential art narration: the limited space for verbal text in the standard comic-book panel makes extensive flashbacks difficult within an ongoing action. In prose Foote can point up the irony of the former gunnery student about to fire on his West Point mentor simply by using a subordinate clause and without disrupting the forward movement of his narrative. But the writer of "April, 1861: Fort Sumter," unable to afford an entire panel for the full story of the old acquaintance yet loath to abandon the telling coincidence entirely, must settle for a paratactic compression that renders Anderson's words comically cryptic. Are we to understand that Anderson would not have discussed the surrender terms with his staff had the Confederate commander been a stranger to him or that Beauregard's quality as a student will somehow affect the negotiations, that perhaps if Beauregard had failed the class in siege tactics the Federals might be well advised to take their chances? The anecdote itself is indeed relevant to the looming internecine conflict, but a single dialogue balloon is too small to allow it the treatment it deserves.

The shift in visual perspective in the third panel serves to undercut the weakness suggested in the verbal text. Anderson has agreed to surrender in three days, but the low-angle view turns him into an imposing and heroic figure, while the sentry to his left strongly supports him. Anderson directly confronts the reader, just as the sentry does in the panel above, and the terseness of his reply, his grim, slightly open mouth, and the official-looking mechanical type make his statement seem less like a capitulation than a challenge, which is how the Confederate envoy takes it in the next panel.[13] Here again the visuals mitigate the overt threat to Anderson and his men. Even though the Confederate in the middle is slightly above the Federal commander, and the officer on the left leans forward in a gesture of menace, Anderson's classically martial pose, anchored by his right hand on the table, and his imperturbable profile both communicate without words his rejection of the Confederate demands. If that profile looks familiar, it should: Anderson's nose, chin, and hairline resemble a reversed image of the face on the Lincoln penny. The Federals need not worry whether "Lincoln has sent reinforcements," this image suggests, because Lincoln's surrogate is already here. The many words in the balloon hover mostly over the Confederates, while the cut-in section of the balloon partially relieves the pressure on the figure of Anderson himself; the crucial words of the conference do not oppress the Union commander despite their visual and symbolic weightiness.

The four-panel sequence concerning the negotiations shares an important historiographic assumption with Shelby Foote's narrative: the activities of the governmental emissaries determined the outbreak of the Civil War. Here history is made by men with official titles, in conferences arranged by rules of order, and its crucial events proceed according to rational arrangements. The *Classics Illustrated* story emphasizes this methodical movement of history in the first panel on the next page (figure 2) by returning back down the chain of command to the "enlisted men who slept near Fort Sumter's guns." The officer's words both warn of the impending attack and temper its dangers, since the garrison can afford to delay its defense until morning. The massive cannon which dominates the panel solidly grounds the visual composition and provides mute evidence of the fort's potential power, while the configuration of the officer's arms is a concrete image of the symbolic authority connecting the prone soldier to the looming instrument of war.

While most of artist Jack Kirby's panel compositions in this sequence focus our attention on the actions inside the panels themselves, the breakdowns on the second page of our example suggest a visual connection between the two top panels, a subtextual link which both enforces and undercuts the literal level of the narrative. The second panel depicts the climactic moment of the entire story, the explosion of the first shot, and the directional line from the left indicating the shell's trajectory leads our attention back to the previous panel, where we find, at almost the exactly appropriate angle, a gun barrel that might have fired that shot.[14]

Thus sequential art does what prose inherently cannot do; it supplies a visual and immediate image of cause (gun) followed by effect (explosion). But at the same time, other visual cues as well as the verbal text tell us that this apparent causality is a false one. The panel border itself signals us to expect a break in time and space, and in the second panel our point of view indeed shifts outside the fort. In addition, the text of the previous panel establishes that this particular gun will *not* fire; in fact, the shot appears to come from the very words "not return fire." The narrative flow requires that the

Figure 2. Jack Kirby, "April, 1861: Fort Sumter," page 3
© The Frawley Corporation

shot be understood as the act of "a Confederate gun crew on James Island" firing an unseen mortar, with no relation to the huge Union cannon which only seems to be pointing into the next panel.

This compositional sleight-of-hand is one of the unique features of sequential art narratives, one that helps distinguish comics from simple illustrated texts. A comic-book artist can thus have it both ways, using the necessary contiguity of panels to create suggestive but subliminal connections which need not correspond to the linear logic of the narrative sequence. In many comic books these image patterns are often more fortuitous than intentional (though no less suggestive), since page and panel layouts are subject routinely to changes by editors in order to accommodate advertisements, pages of fan letters, and other contingencies of mass publication. But in other comics, like the ones with which we are concerned here, creative control over layouts can be much more complete. In this case, the Gilberton Company's line of comic books always used only in-house ads for their publications, so Kirby's effects here are probably deliberate strategies; throughout his long career Jack Kirby's work shows his strong awareness of the compositional role of a comic-book page as a whole.[15]

The crucial panel of the first shot itself contains the most kinetic action of this entire sequence, but even here the impact of the explosion is visually less striking than the bulky mass and apparent invulnerability of Fort Sumter. Kirby's renderings of all the scenes in this story are uncharacteristically static and blocky, utterly unlike the fluid style of high-speed action and anatomic exaggeration which brought him fame in superhero comics such as *Captain America* and *The Fantastic Four*. But this minimizing of tension and violence is not a stylistic slipup by the artist; it is instead an integral part of the ideological thrust of this comic book as a whole. The comic book *War Between the States* was published in 1961 and was one of the many by-products of the national observance of the Civil War centennial. As such it reflects the cultural ambivalence such a celebration perhaps inevitably entails; the visual perspective on this first shot is emblematic of the way narrative choices can be imposed by the search for a societal consensus about the past.

In the early 1960s racial tension and other issues aroused by national desegregation made the Civil War a potentially divisive historical crux, and the writers of this story risked alienating large parts of their audience if they mishandled this watershed event. They did not. Readers see the shot not as the Union garrison sees it nor as the

Confederate gunners see it but from an intermediate and neutral vantage point outside Fort Sumter but much closer to it than any attacker can be. We see as well that no part of the shell burst actually touches the fort, that apparently no person is injured, and that the guns on the fort's lower tier of windowlike casemates are sheltered and ready to reply. In addition, the framing of the panel crops out the flagpole flying the United States flag located just to the left of the panel border, a detail prominent in contemporaneous engravings of the entire fort.[16] The panels leading up to this event do stress the strength and stability of the Federal government (through its military representatives), but at the climactic moment the narrative refuses to indict the rebellious attackers by arousing our anxiety about the fort and its garrison, by showing the emotion-charged image of firing on the flag, or by giving us the viewpoint of one side of the conflict or the other.[17]

The delicate ideological balancing act under way in this comic book is perhaps most evident when we contrast the next panel with the corresponding scene in Foote's account. Both narratives make an identical shift in time and in focus just after the first shot, going from 4:30 A.M. to sunrise and from the opposing military forces to the citizens of Charleston watching from the harborside rooftops. But this point of closest structural correspondence is also where the two versions diverge most radically in their renderings of the historical events. The scene in Foote's passage is manifestly one of civilian martial ardor, as the bellicose South Carolinians "watched from rooftops as from grandstand seats at a fireworks display, cheering." But the narrator of "April, 1861: Fort Sumter" contradicts that account, flatly stating, "Many persons wept." Of course, these opposing versions are not mutually exclusive, since intuition suggests that on that day in that place many indeed cheered while many wept.

The choice between these alternatives is an ideological decision as well as a narrative one (as the action of including both of them would be). Foote's is a traditional American genre scene, the circus or the county fair, featuring "people who had come from miles around by train and buggy, on horseback and afoot, to see the show." Foote's narrative shift to the spectators in Charleston completes the prose account's movement toward the Southern point of view, and so this representation is of a piece with his other narrative choices. Here the long-awaited war is at last under way, and like the cannoneer Edmund Ruffin, these Southerners have no doubt that it will be a quick and glorious validation of Southern superiority.

In the prose account, ambivalence about the war, which Foote attributes to Major Anderson and to Roger Pryor, is seen as a form of emotional weakness; in the political context established in the *Classics Illustrated* story it shows in the Southerners an awareness of the tremendous social and moral consequences of the attack on Fort Sumter. The comic-book panel presents not one but two scenes: far in the background, so far that no details of conflict can be seen, cloudlike shapes rise to the right and left of the tiny structure in the middle of the bay. Without the accompanying narrative context, the scene would be more idyllic than warlike, especially with the dawn pink sweep of sky in the original colored panel.[18] In the foreground several people on rooftops peer anxiously at the faraway vista while others assume classic poses of grief. Together the words and pictures deliver a clear message: these Southerners regret the start of the Civil War. In this panel the narrative generates sympathy for the attackers as human beings without justifying their political cause.

At this crux we might ask for objective historical certainty: were the South Carolinians on the rooftops that day "really" cocksure rubberneckers, as Foote's account suggests, or were they "actually" the anxious souls filled with a dread of a frightening future whom we see in the comic-book panel? The answer is probably both, though to pose the question this way is to ask for a history without a story, for a telling of past events without a reading of them. But we have access to these events only through narrations of them, and as we see in these two versions of history, structural moves in telling a story are interpretive moves as well.

Since no narrative history can transcend interpretation, perhaps a more fruitful question to ask is: *why* are these stories told the way they are, and what social implications do their narrative choices entail? One way to approach these questions is to consider the likely audience for each of these histories and the steps each takes to avoid offending its readers while acknowledging the divisiveness of the American Civil War.

Shelby Foote's audience is a general adult readership, presumably one interested in military history. *The Civil War: A Narrative* follows a tradition in Civil War historiography which emphasizes present-day national unity, downplaying the violent defeat of the Southern bid for political independence while highlighting the military skill of both Union and Confederate soldiers.[19] One of Foote's characteristic strategies throughout his history is to valorize the combatants on both sides by stressing the unprecedented violence and destructiveness of the Civil War, as when, for example, he takes two of his chapter titles from Confederate General Bedford Forrest's grim dictum, "War means fighting. And fighting means killing." Other sections of the full-length history dwell on the new technology of war and the resultant enormous casualty lists.[20]

A corollary to this glorification of the fighters in the war is the deprecation of the militarily ignorant noncombatants. Though told from the Southern point of view, the Fort Sumter passage implicitly contrasts the civilian spectators' naive enthusiasm for this artillery fire with our own knowledge in hindsight of the carnage which ensued after April 1861; these people trivialize the start of what will become an apocalyptic conflict as "a fireworks display." The overall thrust of Foote's narrative, as of much military history, is to present war as ennobling in itself, as a brotherhood of arms which transcends the political or ideological impulses which motivate the combat.[21] The moral, social, and economic ramifications of such an attitude toward warfare are beyond the scope of the present discussion, but it is germane to say that the conception of combat as a cauldron of personal purification, a martial ordeal by fire, was no doubt a comforting one in 1958, as the world struggled to learn to live under the constant threat of inglorious nuclear annihilation. Foote's depiction of the cheering secessionists at once evokes for us a simpler age of heroic spectacle and reveals to us in an ironic light the tenuous innocence of a culture poised on the brink of a catastrophic modern war.

In either case, Foote's Charlestonians cheer because they have yet to learn what we already know: the war will destroy the Southern way of life they seek to preserve. In the *Classics Illustrated* panel, on the other hand, the citizens weep with the knowledge that the cataclysm is upon them. Their foreknowledge makes them projections in period dress of post–Civil War Southerners as the American consensus needs to see them: aware of the Union's strength and repentant for their rebellion against it. The reading audience's physical vantage point on this scene recapitulates a historical relation between the readers and the characters; our elevated point of view in the panel makes us share their perspective while maintaining our distance above and beyond them. One reason this story chooses to endow the Southerners with our historical hindsight relates to the peculiar cultural role of the Gilberton Company's comic books. The *Classics Illustrated* comics were aimed at school-age children, and they function as quasi-textbooks which attempt to enunciate generally held social values, but they do so in a narrative medium usually rejected as vulgar by the society itself. These comics can afford no enemies, and in telling the story of the American Civil War, this narrative must glorify heroes in a national conflict but may damn no villains.[22] The suffering spectators, their faces averted from us, perhaps in shame, do not threaten the national fabric in the historical past, and their moral awareness at the moment of crisis implies a similar ethical consciousness on the part of their present-day heirs.

A visual narrative of this scene which depicted a boisterous mob gloating at the assault on the Stars and Stripes would be well within the bounds of "historical accuracy," but this comic-book panel scrupulously avoids such inflammatory images, stressing instead to its young readers that the Confederate citizens do not attack Fort Sumter with naive optimism or belligerent glee (as Foote's description might suggest); rather, they feel fully the pangs of conscience for their revolutionary acts.[23] Foote can afford to exploit the irony implicit in the scene of the Charlestonians, who cheer at the onset of the deluge, without alienating the Southerners in his audience because his narrative is, on the whole, sympathetic to the Confederate cause. He explains this manifest partiality in nonpolitical terms as "the average American's normal sympathy for the underdog in a fight."[24] But as an attempt to articulate a national consensus view of history, the *Classics Illustrated* narrative cannot divorce the war from politics. It must ratify the present-day political and social consequences of the Northern triumph in the Civil War, and the sympathy the panels generate for the Rebels, so necessary for the appearance of ideological evenhandedness, finally reinforces rather than undercuts the validity of the Union victory.

If the panel of the exploding first shot is from a neutral vantage point, and the panel of the Southern spectators shows the scene which they see, the final panel of this example moves firmly back to the Union point of view. The medium close-up of Major Anderson and Captain Doubleday presents them as large, solidly grounded figures, and the wall in the background shields them from the shells exploding just outside. These two men seem almost magically oblivious to the shell burst—or even more: the explosion forms a kind of halo around Doubleday's head, a corona of power radiating from his round officer's hat. The explosion behind his head is also placed directly below the very similar image of the first shot in the panel just above it, although here the image lacks the sinister ring of black smoke. The complex visual configuration which links the first shot to this panel—Anderson's verbal order to Doubleday's saluting arm and Doubleday's head to the explosion—suggests that the Rebel attack, so far from being a threat to the high-walled fort, has instead endowed its defenders with a divine energy.

The very texture of the lines in this panel associates the men and the fort with the power of the explosion; Doubleday's right arm and belt, Anderson's hat and shoulder, and the floor and wall behind them are all composed of the same parallel sketchy lines as the image of the shell burst itself. The heavy shading of Anderson, his half-turned posture, our viewpoint directly over his shoulder, the statement in the dialogue balloon, and the formal introduction in the caption all combine to focus attention on the figure of Captain Abner Doubleday. His nimbus of glory is an appropriate crown for a secular American saint: this grim-faced military subordinate is also the legendary inventor of the game of baseball.

The concentration on Doubleday in this narrative (Foote never mentions him) emphasizes a perhaps startling historical synchronism: one of the central participants in the originating event of the Civil War was also the originator of the game that has come to mean America to the world. The narrative never directly mentions Doubleday's purported achievement. If readers know enough baseball lore to associate this figure with the national pastime, such all-American connotations help suggest the ways in which the Civil War and its participants formed our own contemporary American culture. If they do not, the panel itself reaffirms the strength of the fort and the determination of its defenders, and it also invokes the authority of the military chain of command which began this two-page sequence.

The panel breakdowns of the entire second page form a cycle which moves forward in time but returns to its starting place in space just inside the walls of Fort Sumter. In doing so the page exploits the inherently dialectical nature of sequential art narrations. The linearity of the verbal elements enforces the temporal movement of the narrative; each caption begins by marking the time: "As the Confederate officers rowed away," "At 4:30," "By sunrise," and "A few minutes before seven." On the other hand, the visual elements need not likewise progress in space, and when the point of view does shift places, it need not make the same moves as the verbal text. Here the visual return to the fort counteracts any political or moral uncertainty generated by the two-panel shift in viewpoint to the exterior of the fort and to the (highly qualified) Confederate view.

It is obvious that prose must be read in a linear, time-based sequence, while pictures can be experienced at once, but the peculiar and wonderfully versatile dialectic of sequential art is that in comic strips and comic books both verbal and visual elements can work both sequentially and simultaneously. Words are indeed set in a fixed order, but captions, dialogue in balloons, and, as we shall see, most especially sound effects all perform important compositional as well as linguistic functions. We experience panels in comics at once and in any order, but as narrative elements they presuppose a left-to-right and top-to-bottom (that is, a reading) order. Panel compositions also create thematic and narrative relations which can be characterized only as grammatical and syntactical. In addition, an important class of pictures operates primarily as word surrogates: visual puns (for example, light bulb = idea), cultural icons, and any pictorial representations which are "verbalized" by being placed in a dialogue balloon or a caption space all function only when translated into verbal terms.

Sequential art is not the only medium to use words and pictures, of course, but analogies with other media can obscure as much as they reveal about comics. The shifting viewpoints of the panels resemble camera cuts in cinema, but unlike the moviegoer, the comic-book reader can partially anticipate and control the pace and order of the changes. Verbal captions and dialogue help the *Classics Illustrated* comic to approximate the linear movement of Foote's prose passage, but the combination of words and pictures demands a different order of perception from that required by a page of prose. Comic panels at first resemble illustrated texts or captioned pictures, but the relation of the two elements is much more intimate and problematical in comics than in a news photograph or a novel with pictures. The synthesis of words and pictures in comic books finally becomes a narrative gestalt combining verbal movement and sequence with pictorial stasis and simultaneity, and vice versa. The elements of sequential art are separable for our analytic convenience, but they are kept apart only at the cost of the visceral power and expressive range of the medium.

Relatively few of the special techniques available to sequential art narrations are deployed in "April, 1861: Fort Sumter." Here are none of the onomatopoetic sound effects so familiar in comics, no thought balloons (two of the eight panels have no balloons at all), no nonrectangular or open-bordered panels, and no intrusion of the text into the pictorial space. But artist Jack Kirby used all these devices in other comics, some so boldly and so often as to make them his trademarks. This refusal to use many of the conventional stylistic gestures of the medium indicates the essentially defensive stance of this history: defense against potential charges of historical bias by sectional partisans, as we have seen, but defense also against hostile media critics, such as anti-comic-book crusader Dr. Fredric Wertham, for whom comic books are inherently sensational, trivial, and illiterate. This narrative's characteristic strategies demonstrate an attempt to produce a comic book as little like a typical comic book as possible while still exploiting the form's storytelling potential.[25] The result is a history that is as clear and plausible as Foote's prose account and a comic book that is at once evocative in its presentation and restrained in its narrative.

Such restraint accounts as well for the stolid pace of these comic-book pages: the verbal rhythm of the captions is so measured as to be monotonous, the panels, though well composed, are static, and the rendering of the figures is a bit stiff. The stylistic rigidity of the *Classics Illustrated* history points to a narrative suspended between the pull of two opposing audiences, each with its own contrasting demands and expectations, and both vital to the economic survival of the Gilberton Company's didactic project. The eventual readers of the *Classics Illustrated* comics were elementary school students, and these educational comics had to compete for the attention of young readers with the full range of superhero, horror, adventure, war, humor, and romance comics. The comic-book form was chosen by the Gilberton Company for the "purpose of 'wooing' youngsters to great books."[26]

But if children did not choose to read classic literature and history in book form, they were likewise unlikely to embrace edification simply because it came equipped with panels and dialogue balloons. The *Classics Illustrated* comics therefore required the goodwill and support of an adult audience, not as readers, but as intermediate purchasers. Comic books faced increasing cultural hostility in the late 1940s and early 1950s because of the violence and sensationalism of many of them, and for a time the suppression of all comic books seemed a real possibility.[27] In response, the Gilberton Company attempted to distinguish its books from less high-minded comics and to create a more "cultured" image for its products by changing the format of its comic books in 1951 from cheap paper and line-drawn cover art to heavier stock and painted covers. The resulting price increase took the *Classics* beyond the average juvenile budget. For example, in 1961 *The War Between the States* cost thirty-five cents, three and one-half times as much as each new *Batman, Uncle Scrooge,* or any of the other comic-book competitors.

The marketing of such an expensive product required that parents and educators buy the *Classics* for their children and students. Each *Classics Illustrated* comic therefore had to try to reconcile the pressures brought to bear by the two parts of its audience: the kids who read them wanted exciting stories, not extracurricular education; the adults who bought them wanted respectable literature for their young charges but tended to lump all comic books together as pernicious and subliterary trash. No wonder then if "April, 1861: Fort Sumter" creaks from the strain; the surprise is that the *Classics* were able to maintain alone the premise of serious literature in comic-book form for so long and that they did it so well.

Always queer hybrids of the popular and the highbrow, the *Classics Illustrated* comics seemed at times to be pretentious poor relations in the library and stodgy dowager queens on the newsstands. The faint whiff of absurdity clings to the roots of their paradoxical enterprise. Their goal was to encourage young readers to grow beyond their infatuation with comic books to a love of "real" literature, to read Shelby Foote rather than Jack Kirby. They expressed their loyalty finally to the canonical prose texts of the high culture, and the carefully researched and scrupulously presented products of the Gilberton Company cannot disguise at last that their essential endeavor is to make themselves obsolete.

E.C.'s Two-Fisted Pacifism

The four-color bêtes noires of the proponents of genteel comics and of the anti-comic-book zealots alike were the often grisly and always wildly imaginative E.C. lines of horror, fantasy, crime, and science fiction comics, all written by editor Al Feldstein. Even publisher William Gaines was hard-pressed to persuade an unsympathetic congressional committee in 1954 of the redeeming social value of such blood-spattered E.C. offerings as "Foul Play," in which a baseball pitcher is murdered by an opposing team and pieces of his dismembered corpse are used as equipment in a macabre midnight baseball game.[20] The E.C. war comics, with writing, layouts, and often finished art by editor Harvey Kurtzman, featured no such extravaganzas of graphic gore.[29] They were instead the first antiwar war comics in the history of the medium, and the splash page from "First Shot," shown in figure 3, illustrates both Kurtzman's commitment to traditional standards of historical accuracy and his determination to produce works which would, in his words, show "the utter horror and futility of war."[30]

Even more strongly than either Shelby Foote's Civil War narrative or the *Classics Illustrated* story, the splash page of "First Shot" insists on the historical importance of the cannon shot itself. The bold-lettered title, the breathless verbal narrative, and the detailed close-ups of the mortar shell's firing, flight, and explosion assert that this specific incident is of profound significance as an originating event. But the emphasis here on the physical particulars of the shot suggests a radical difference between the E.C. story and the other two versions. Foote and Kirby both show how the actions of prominent men brought about the American Civil War; Harvey Kurtzman shows history in the act of escaping from human control. Instead of a prearranged event in a rational, chronological sequence, we see in these panels a disruption, a bursting forth of an overwhelming and inhuman power. Unlike Edmund Ruffin and Major Anderson, the men around this cannon do not start the Civil War; rather, the war is a thing which happens *to* them.

Where "April, 1861: Fort Sumter" downplayed both the images of direct conflict in its story and the technical idiosyncrasies of its sequential art form, "First Shot" stresses the materiality of the comic-book page, an appropriate emphasis for a narrative sequence which concentrates on the impersonal objects of war.[31] The *Classics* comic used ruled and typeset dialogue balloons, bracketing off the words from the pictures in order to bring its problematic ideological tensions under control. The E.C. page eschews dialogue balloons altogether in favor of sound effects drawn directly within the panels; the most forceful speaker in this sequence is the cannonball itself. The words of the other speaker, the narrative voice, are likewise not confined to caption boxes. In the large panel the captions share the pictorial space (the title is a major compositional element), while in the lower tier they occupy an intermediate area outside the panels but not separated from one another by borderlines.

The page thus physically integrates two widely disparate narrative strains: the visual elements, which dominate the page, show in five panels an event lasting a few seconds at most; the verbal text sets

Figure 3. Harvey Kurtzman, John Severin, and Will Elder, "First Shot," page 1
© 1952 by Tiny Tot, Comics, Inc.; renewed © 1980 by William M. Gaines, Agent

the physical scene ("in Charleston Harbor") and relates the shot to a wider temporal ("a month back") and political context. Together the words and pictures of this sequence overtly present the political issues buried or repressed in the *Classics* version. The clear sight of the two opposing flags prohibits our neutrality about the shot; the threat to the vulnerable fort (sitting "like an orphan duck") is obvious; and the bursting shell is neither essentially ceremonial, as Foote's prose suggests, nor harmless, as Kirby's drawing shows it, but instead a real act of violence carrying dire social and individual consequences as it explodes in the reader's face.

The splash panel is at once more precisely detailed and much more dynamic than any single panel of the *Classics* sequence. The sandbags and barrels which surround the gun emplacement, the floating "water battery" with its Confederate flag in the left middle ground, the long shot of Fort Sumter in the background beyond the oppressive smoke cloud, and the civilian dress and contorted postures of the human figures all portray in a single frame the physical and political relations of the opposing forces. But here the visual subtext belies the seeming simplicity of the terms of the conflict. True, the Confederates are firing on the Union fort, but the rebels themselves are being traumatized by their act: they must shield their eyes and ears from the long-awaited yet unexpected violence, and the debris flying from the cannon threatens to strike them. The high-trajectory mortar barrel does not even seem to be pointing at the fort (though the observers to the lower left are looking in that direction) but instead shoots straight up into the sky, as if attacking the omniscient narrative voice.

The shot's flame and smoke create a dominating image which serves to move the splash panel beyond its immediate context as a telling of the past to suggest subliminally the relevance of this comic book to its own historical situation: the shot from this 1861 smoothbore siege mortar replicates the familiar and sinister mushroom cloud of the atomic bomb. Like much of American culture in the 1950s, the E.C. comics were fascinated to the point of obsession with the ramifications of life in the shadow of the atomic bomb. Two of E.C.'s finest stories show in graphic detail the horrific effects of atomic warfare, in the genres of science fiction ("There Will Come Soft Rains," an adaptation of Ray Bradbury's short story of the same name) and history (Kurtzman's story of Nagasaki, "Atomic Bomb").[32] The E.C. comics were as committed to raising the questions of the atomic age as the Gilberton comics were to suppressing them; "First Shot" exploits the connotations of its images to assert the importance of a single projectile on the course of history without resorting to the distancing devices of the *Classics Illustrated* story.

The connection between Civil War history and 1950s America becomes even closer in this context when we remember that the United States was involved in 1952 in another North-South internecine conflict: the Korean War, where the country which had struggled so fiercely for its own unification found itself fighting to maintain a schism in the middle of a foreign nation. The war in Korea supplied the material for most of Kurtzman's war stories; *Frontline Combat* and *Two-Fisted Tales* featured notable stories from a variety of historical periods, but the Korean War stories outnumbered all the others by at least three to one. The special issues on the Civil War were bracketed by issues in which the ongoing Korean conflict was the thematic focus, as the loyal readers of E.C. comics were well aware, and both Korea and atomic anxiety were never far from any E.C. war comic page, both literally and figuratively.

While the events depicted in the *Classics Illustrated* "April, 1861: Fort Sumter" serve to reinforce the stability of the 1961 American commonweal, the first page of "First Shot" evokes past events as analogues to the crises of its 1952 present; the ballistic arc so fully delineated here was, or was soon to become, a shorthand sign for Armageddon.[33] The bottom tier of panels demonstrates a distinctive technique of comic-book art in the hands of one of the form's masters: a brief action is broken down into quick segments and viewed from shifting perspectives. The relationship between the splash panel and the first panel of the second tier is ambiguous. The height of the cannonball when we first see it suggests that the action cannot take place long after the firing, yet either the men have already turned back toward the gun (unlikely in such a brief time) or they have not yet turned away, which places the second panel chronologically *before* the first; either way the two panels come close to being simultaneous views of a single event.[34]

The viewpoint of the first small panel puts the reader in the place of the narrative voice of the splash panel (or of God), and the sound effect ("BWOWM!") both physically supports the ball and links the panel to the next by crossing the panel border; the round ball of the exclamation point repeats the shape of the shell as it starts its descending arc. The reader's perspective in the next panel moves closer to the target, and the ball becomes more threatening; the sound effect ("SKREeeeee") leads the eye back along the shot's trajectory to the scene established in the splash panel. The third panel in the second tier shows Fort Sumter as we never saw it in the *Classics Illustrated* pages: where Kirby's drawings stressed the strength and stability of the fort's walls, the E.C. panel shows the "dark pentagon" which Foote describes,[35] open from above and vulnerable to the steeply plunging Confederate shell heading directly for the American flag. The perspective shifts back to a point above the ball; the "EEEE" sound effect continues the screech of the previous panel as the shell draws nearer to the fort, which seems especially threatened since the fort and the ball are of precisely the same size. In the climactic final panel the conspicuous role of the sound effects in this sequence culminates as the word "BLAM!" obliterates the scene entirely. The lines of force, smoke, and debris in the panel surround the sound effect and suggest a blinding vision of apocalypse, completing the pattern of connotations begun by the mushroom cloud in the splash panel.

The verbal text on this page, though its primary focus is far removed in time from the visual narrative, reinforces the thematic suggestions of the pictures. In the splash panel the caption serves the expository function of invoking the name of the fort and placing it in Charleston Harbor, but the main power of the text is its incantatory string of similes: "like a rock," "like a red hot potato," "like an orphan duck," and "a box," while the capital H of "SHOT" repeats the columnar barrel shape of the exploding mortar directly below it. In the lower tier, the first and last panels essentially repeat the information shown in the pictures, while the middle two sketch in the terms of the conflict. In contrast to the irresolution of Major Anderson in Foote's account, here the resolve of "Lincoln's boys" causes the opening shot of the conflict. The sound effects in each of the lower panels are at least as important as the more formal sentences in the captions, and they do far more: they function both as words which reproduce sounds and as major design elements in the pictures.

The letters of "BWOWM!" and "BLAM!" overlap one another, approximating the percussive quality of the explosions they represent, while the letters of the shell's screech grow larger as the shot approaches the reader's vantage point, visually suggesting the sound variations of the moving cannonball. Kurtzman here fully exploits the range of sequential art conventions which the Kirby pages so carefully avoid. The exclamatory chant of the verbal narration, the brisk pace of the panel breakdowns, and the graphic violence of the shot's explosion combine to create a more frenzied and kinetic effect than the *Classics Illustrated* comic's stately movement and distant tone.

The splash page of "First Shot" encapsulates several of the ideological tensions of the *Frontline Combat* series. Like many of the Korean War stories which surrounded the Civil War issues, the page evokes the awesome power of the technology of destruction and demonstrates the subordination of the human to the mechanical in modern warfare. This ubiquitous E.C. theme is stated most forcefully in Kurtzman's story "How They Die," in which a maimed French veteran of World War I characterizes advancing American soldiers as "servants of the machine"; he limps home in the final panel, musing, "Perhaps now that war is fought by terrible machines and man realizes that he is committing suicide, wars will end!"[36] But America's relation to war and its machines has always been ambivalent: these Confederate gunners reel in terror from the altar of the war god, yet the conflict begun here eventually leads to a unified America and freedom for the slaves, a result implicitly approved in the story preceding "First Shot" in *Frontline Combat* no. 9, "Abe Lincoln."

While the flaming mortar and its sinister cannonball dominate the fates of the human beings on this page, other E.C. war stories celebrate the lifesaving capabilities of America's war technology.[37] Like the *Classics Illustrated* comics, *Two-Fisted Tales* and *Frontline Combat* contain their own paradox: antiwar war comics must make their subject repulsive yet fascinating enough to read about. Though opposed to war in general, they depend on war for their existence.

In fact, the end of the Korean War in 1954 spelled the doom of *Frontline Combat;* the once hard-hitting *Two-Fisted Tales* survived as a rather tepid adventure comic. The grimly pacifistic message of both books was never popular with American comic-book readers; despite the consummate craftsmanship of the E.C. staff and Harvey Kurtzman's unflinching editorial vision, the war comics never sold enough copies to pay their way, and only twelve of the projected twenty-eight Civil War stories were ever published.[38] The splash page of "First Shot" demonstrates Kurtzman's skill in using the special conventions of the comic-book form: the precise and detailed page layout, the dynamic lower tier with its individual panels adroitly linked by sound effects and visual perspective, the dramatic final panel, the neatly integrated verbal text. But its powerful narrative finally presents an unwelcome vision of history; Americans were reluctant to hear that their obsession with technology was suicidal and threatened the world with destruction.

"First Shot," like Kurtzman's other E.C. war stories, combines the twin impulses in historical comic books of didacticism and sensationalism: the story is consistent with the historical record and is forcefully, almost feverishly rendered in both words and pictures.[39] The radical contrasts among Shelby Foote's prose account of the first shot at Fort Sumter, the *Classics* "April 1861: Fort Sumter," and E.C.'s "First Shot" do not originate in differences of artistic quality, factual accuracy, or storytelling skill. Yet the three narratives diverge so sharply as to render problematic the notion that they depict the "same event" at all. Each version exploits differing formal strategies for divergent ideological ends: Foote takes advantage of the linearity of prose to emphasize the chronological sequence of events, and the regular movement of his narrative through time masks its subtle shifts toward the Southern point of view; in *The Civil War: A Narrative*, the first shot is an act accomplished by the Confederates. The *Classics Illustrated* story gives essentially the same verbal information as Foote but with a very different impetus, using the visual text to assert that the shot is successfully resisted by the Federal forces inside the fort. The splash page of Kurtzman's story shows both sides of the military struggle at the mercy of the shot itself, stressing the implacable and mechanical force of history.

A comparison between Foote's account and "April, 1861: Fort Sumter" suggests that prose can present information such as times and dates more effectively and can make temporal shifts more elegantly than can sequential art; in the panel breakdowns of the *Classics Illustrated* pages a movement forward in time requires a similar movement in space; the comic's attempt at a flashback within a panel (Anderson's memory of Beauregard as a student) is maladroit at best. What the comic book *can* do which the prose alone cannot is to show in space the relations of the physical elements of the story (the Charlestonians and the fort, for example), and it can keep previous scenes physically before the reader after the narrative has moved on (as in the doubled explosions of the first shot and the bursting halo behind Abner Doubleday); the images are at once more immediate and more subliminal than in prose. Pictures might seem to leave less to the imagination than do words, but the narrative leaps we are required to make between the panels of a comic-book story, as well as the semiotic reading necessary to decode the lines, colors, and verbal text in a sequential art page give an attentive comic-book reader quite enough to do.

The two comic-book treatments of the first shot at Fort Sumter exhibit contrasting conceptions of the rhythm of comic-book narrative. The solemn tone and logical panel shifts of the *Classics Illustrated* pages solidly ground the story's action and minimize the reader's anxiety about a culturally traumatic event. The E.C. page uses its frantic verbal pace, compulsive similemaking, and quick, disconcerting jumps in point of view to heighten that same anxiety. In "First Shot," the conspicuous verbal/visual role of the shot's sound effects epitomizes that blending of word and image which distinguishes sequential art as a literary medium. Because of their educational function, the *Classics Illustrated* pages are less self-assured about their comic-book form, so they segregate the words and pictures and eschew sound effects entirely. Both these examples omit a wide range of narrative devices and stylistic tricks available in sequential art: dialogue configurations in comics are usually much more complex than the one balloon per panel in "April, 1861: Fort Sumter," panel shapes and sizes can be much more various than we see in either example, and the style of rendering in both comics is relatively conservative and straightforward.

As always in historical storytelling, the stylistic choices in these comic books are likewise ideological ones. Kirby's pages show his enormous artistic vitality held in check by his didactic purpose; Kurtzman's narrative vigor serves to attack war itself. These pages do what American comic-book stories do not often attempt: they claim to tell a true story of the past, and such stories can never be told from some neutral vantage point which is beyond politics. The connection of comic books and politics is an uncomfortable one in America—comics have for so long been the province of juvenile adventure and innocuous humor. But as these examples should demonstrate, the thematic puerility and wholesale fantasy of commercial comic books are not functions of the sequential art medium itself.

Comic books can and have been used as the vehicles for scrupulously accurate history and realistic fiction and for politically committed narratives which make overt their ideological dimensions. But such comics have had to be written outside the mainstream of comic-book publishing; the surge of public feeling against comic books in the 1950s led to such severe censorship that comics became perforce fit for children—and only for children. The E.C.

comics disappeared (with one exception), and not until the emergence of the underground comics of the 1960s would there again appear in America comic books which combined the narrative drive and thematic high seriousness of comics such as Harvey Kurtzman's E.C. war comics.

But *Frontline Combat* and *Two-Fisted Tales* were not direct victims of the Comics Code; they folded in part because William Gaines transferred Harvey Kurtzman from the war comics to a very different project—one which resulted in the most influential magazine in comic-book history, E.C.'s only survivor of the Comics Code debacle, and a continuing role model for America's mildly rebellious youth: the parody comic book *Mad*. The tradition of comic-book humor which *Mad* exemplifies lies at the margins of the present discussion of comic-book treatments of history, but *Mad* is a crucial element in the cultural mix which eventually resulted in the underground comics explosion of the 1960s, which in turn gave rise to the more widely accepted works of Harvey Pekar, Art Spiegelman, and Jack Jackson in the 1980s. Many of the underground artists were just old enough to remember the pre–Comics Code E.C. comics and all grew up at a time when the sharpest satire of American culture was found each month in the pages of the magazine-sized *Mad*. It is something more than a coincidence that the contemporary comic-book genres of freewheeling social satire and ideologically committed historical narratives both found their earliest and most powerful form in the work of Harvey Kurtzman.[40]

1. These examples and those below can be found in Robert Overstreet, *The Comic Book Price Guide* (Cleveland, Tenn.: Harmony Books, annual).

2. Michael Sawyer, "Albert Lewis Kanter and the Classics: The Man behind the Gilberton Company," *Journal of Popular Culture* 20 (1987): 13.

3. *Code of the Comics Magazine Association of America*, Preamble (n.p., 1954).

4. The E.C. Civil War series was prepared with the assistance of the popular historian Fletcher Pratt.

5. The examples are: a section of the first chapter of Shelby Foote's *The Civil War: A Narrative* (New York: Random House, 1958), 1:48–49; two pages from "April, 1861: Fort Sumter" in *The War Between the States, Classics Illustrated Special Issue* no. 162a (June 1961); and the first page of "First Shot," from E.C.'s *Frontline Combat* no. 9 (November–December 1952).

6. These two poles of historical narration are stated succinctly in a recent prospectus for a military history periodical, which promises to "hire first-rate writers, the kind that get their facts right *and* bring past events to vivid, thrilling life" Prospectus for *Military History Quarterly* (New York [?] n.p., n.d.).

7. Foote, *Civil War*, 1:48–49.

8. A "splash" page is often a full-page drawing which introduces a comic-book

story. The term is also used to describe oversized panels, as in the E.C. discussion below, and for large panels which take up one or more pages ("one- or two-page splash").

9. See, for example, Kirby's art on page 4 of "The Invasion of Asgard" in *Journey into Mystery* no. 101 (February 1964), where the drastic leaps in time and perspective create a frantically paced and difficult-to-follow fight scene.

10. The best discussion of the conventions of sequential art can be found in Lawrence L. Abbott, "Comic Art: Characteristics and Potentialities of a Narrative Medium," *Journal of Popular Culture* 19 (1986): 155–173.

11. The E.C. comics, and probably the Gilberton comics as well, used a stenciling system called Leroy lettering, which consists of a penholder and a template of letters and symbols for the artist to follow. Leroy letters are used mainly in engineering drafting.

12. Will Eisner, *Sequential Art*, 27.

13. The blank background and the sentry's hooded eyes also focus our attention on Anderson's face and his imposing upper torso rather than on the speech balloon.

14. We also see the line of sight of the officer in the background leading out of the left-hand panel into the right, as if he is looking at the shot, thus reinforcing the relationship between the panels.

15. In fact, one historian of the comics asserts that "[in *Captain America*] Kirby invented the full-page and double-page comic spread" (Wolfgang Fuchs, in Horn, *World Encyclopedia of Comics*, 429).

16. See, for example, the often reproduced engraving in Horace Greeley, *The American Conflict*, 2 vols. (Hartford: O. D. Case, 1864), 1:440–441.

17. Even the title of the comic, *The War Between the States*, uses a term for the war which attributes responsibility for the conflict evenly, avoiding the connotations of social disruption suggested in the more usual phrase "Civil War" as well as the political special pleading of names such as "War of the Rebellion" and "War for Southern Independence."

18. Because of the impossibility of including color illustrations, I have not undertaken a full discussion here of the narrative role of color in comic books, but color patterns do perform an important function in creating tone and atmosphere.

19. Examples of this tradition can be found throughout the four-volume *Battles and Leaders of the Civil War*, ed. Robert Underwood Johnson and Clarence Clough Buel (New York: Century, 1884–1888).

20. Foote, *Civil War*, 349, 350, 351.

21. Foote's most overt statement of this distinction between combat and politics comes in his "Bibliographical Note," where he says, "I hope I have recovered the respect [the Confederate veterans] had for their opponents until Reconstruction lessened and finally killed it" (Foote, *Civil War*, 816).

22. The *Classics Illustrated* comics were included in the virulent attack on all comic books as causes of juvenile delinquency and social disintegration in Dr. Wertham's *Seduction of the Innocent*, 142–143.

23. For a prose description of this scene as the "exulting revels" of the Southerners, see Greeley, *American Conflict*, 1:447, 449.

24. Foote, *Civil War*, 816.

25. This distancing of the product from the form can be seen most clearly in the change of the series title from *Classic Comics* to *The Classics Illustrated* in 1947. Sawyer, "Gilberton Company," 5.

26. Ibid., 4.

27. For example, New York formed the Joint Legislative Committee on Comic Book Control in 1951, and a similar body held hearings in Albany in 1955.

28. *The Haunt of Fear* no. 19 (May–June 1953).

29. Though he was nominally editor of the E.C. war titles, Kurtzman's control over his comics was unusually complete; his scripts included page breakdowns and detailed thumbnail sketches for each panel. It is no injustice to the artists (here the skilled team of John Severin and Will Elder) to characterize the E.C. war comics as the work of Harvey Kurtzman.

30. Quoted in Daniels, *Comix*, 67. Kurtzman's penchant, indeed mania, for accurate historical details was legendary among E.C. staffers, whom he sent on field trips to libraries, armories, and once on a dive in a submarine to research battles, weapons, and sound effects; an E.C. Christmas greeting featuring caricatures of the staff shows a combat-helmeted Kurtzman demanding, "Now I want you guys to get out there and make them stories real! *REAL YA HEAR!*"

31. This impersonality and distance is suggested, only to be reversed on the next page; most of "First Shot" follows the fortunes of an individual Union soldier inside Fort Sumter. The story makes a thematic full circle on the last page; the protagonist ironically becomes the only casualty of the siege when he is killed by an accidentally exploding cannon, a victim of the blind caprices of war.

32. "There Will Come Soft Rains," *Weird Fantasy* no. 17, (January–February 1953); Bradbury's story is copyright 1950. See "Atom Bomb," *Two-Fisted Tales* no. 33 (May–June 1953).

33. By 1953, less than two years after the publication of "First Shot," both the United States and the Soviet Union possessed thermonuclear weapons and intercontinental attack capabilities.

34. The explosive sound effect also suggests that the lower panel depicts the precise moment of the gun's firing.

35. Foote, *Civil War*, 49.

36. "How They Die," *Frontline Combat* no. 3 (November–December 1951), 7.

37. See, for example, "H-5," in *Frontline Combat* no. 12 (May–June 1953), and "Albatross," in *Frontline Combat* no. 14 (October 1953), both of which feature downed U.S. airmen rescued by specialized American aircraft. Kurtzman has said that one of the "elementary truths" which were the starting points of the war stories is, "'War's battles are fought by men, not machines'" (Harvey Kurtzman, "An Interview with the Man Who Brought Truth to the Comics," interview by Kim Thompson and Gary Groth [Spring 1981], *Comics Journal* 67 [October 1981]:81).

38. Publisher William M. Gaines supported the war titles and allowed the popular E.C. crime and horror titles to counterbalance the war comics' lackluster sales. See William M. Gaines, interview with Dwight Decker and Gary Groth, *Comics Journal* 81 (May 1983):58.

39. The E.C. story is a bit more precise in historical details than the *Classics Illustrated* story, which anachronistically shows the Confederate officers in 1862-style uniforms.

40. Kurtzman's post-*Mad* humor magazine, *Help!*, published the early work of such artists as Robert Crumb, Jay Lynch, and Gilbert Shelton, all of whom later went on to become mainstays of the underground comics scene. Harvey Kurtzman's influence on the undergrounds is discussed in Mark James Estren, *A History of Underground Comics* (San Francisco: Straight Arrow, 1977), 294–300. For a briefer and more recent evaluation, see R. Fiore, "Funnybook Roulette," *Comics Journal* 118 (December 1987):43–46.

2

The Underground Roots of Fact-Based Comics

The Comic-Book Code

E.C.'s *Mad* magazine was able to evade the strictures of the Comics Code only because in 1955 publisher William M. Gaines shifted the format of his biting parodies of American media and social customs from a standard-sized color comic book to a black-and-white magazine. Otherwise the grip of the Code was ironclad; by the late 1950s few comic books were sold in America without the distinctive Comics Code Authority seal of approval.[1] The Comics Code Authority is an independent board established in 1954 by the comic-book industry to review the editorial content of comic books and ensure that they abide by the provisions of the Comics Code, self-proclaimed the "most stringent code in existence for any communications media."[2] The Comics Code established rigid and sweeping rules for the content of comic books: "Guidelines of the authority prohibit displays of corrupt authority, successful crimes, happy criminals, the triumph of evil over good, violence, concealed weapons, the death of a policeman, sensual females, divorce, illicit sexual relations, narcotics or drug addiction, physical afflictions, poor grammar, and the use of the words 'crime,' 'horror,' and 'terror' in the title of a magazine or a story."[3] The nearly universal adoption of the Comics Code is perhaps the single most influential event in the history of the American comic book medium; it efficiently squelched the few postwar comic books that were groping toward a sophisticated audience, and in effect it decreed that all comic books would become the ill-crafted pap toward which most American comics tended anyway.[4] The Comics Code functioned perfectly as an economic instrument of social censorship; magazine distributors, fearful of parental protests, simply refused to handle non-Code-approved books, and dozens of small comic-book publishers folded when they failed to replace their ersatz-E.C. horror and suspense comics with products which were both socially respectable and commercially viable on the newsstands.

Sex, violence, and anarchy in the comics did not disappear after the introduction of the Comics Code, of course; Dr. Wertham, whose inflammatory *Seduction of the Innocent* mobilized the public indignation which spawned the Code, was nonplussed to find in the post-Code comics the same dangerous themes as ever, now, as one writer says, "[disguised] in a hypocritical aura of good taste where the ghastly effects of heartless cruelty were never realistically depicted. Murder looked more like a game than ever under the new self-awarded seal of approval."[5]

But despite the chaos peeking through the new bourgeois clothes, comic books were sorely limited in their narrative and thematic possibilities. The Code's ostensible intent was the protection of young and impressionable readers from graphic violence and celebrations of crime, but its provisions work mainly to quell the vitality of the comics and to ratify authoritarian social control. Along with its rules against "violations of good taste or decency," the Code intones: "Policemen, judges, government officials and respected institutions shall not be presented in such a way as to create disrespect for established authority."[6] The Code's insistence that "good" must always triumph over "evil" fossilized the comics' tendency toward oversimplified conflicts and led to thematic and generic stagnation; it stripped away even the vestiges of plot suspense from the crime and adventure comics, and it damned in one phrase the soul of the horror genre, which requires at least the possibility of evil triumphing over good.[7] Not until the introduction of the psychologically torn "hero-villain" in the Marvel superhero comics of the middle 1960s would a semblance of moral ambiguity return to mainstream comic books; the overt conflicts remained as stereotyped as ever, but soap-opera self-doubt eventually replaced melodramatic self-righteousness as the dominant tone of the comic-book hero.

The final effect of the Comics Code was to force comic books to depict a world that was either a denatured view of American social reality (à la Archie and Jughead) or an overtly fantastic never-never land of superpowered Manichean fisticuffs. Historical narratives in comic book form became nearly impossible; the ban on "all scenes of horror, excessive bloodshed, gory or gruesome crimes, depravity, lust, sadism, [and] masochism" can be taken to rule out nearly everything in the history of Western civilization except inspirational biographies and patriotic exemplum. Of course, the rule forbidding "disrespect for established authority" made political satire nearly impossible.[8]

To bash the Comics Code is easy enough: its patent (and successful) attempt to eliminate specific "undesirable" comics publishers is reprehensible; its naive assumption of the unproblematic nature of terms like "good" and "evil" and "excessive violence" would be laughable were its effects not so repressive of free speech; the bland and tedious comic books it mandated are a literary stigma from which the medium has been hard-pressed to recover.[9] But it is important to remember that the Comics Code was not imposed on the industry by the government. In fact, its provisions make hash of the First Amendment and could stand no legal test. But the Code's rules are not laws; they are self-imposed industry guidelines, and as such they simply codified the existing editorial leanings of most American comics. E.C.'s powerfully written war comics failed because of lagging newsstand sales, not because of the meddling of the Comics Code, and while the Code killed off the most sophisticated American comic books, for many other comics the Code simply meant business as usual. The Code officially ruled out overtly mature treatments of adult themes in American comic books, but few such books had existed before the Code anyway, and to blame only the Comics Code Authority for the lack of serious literature in comics form is badly to underestimate the puerility of the comic book publishers and of the mainstream comics audience.

The Underground Comix

The Code did serve to articulate in an unusually direct and peremptory form the bourgeois artistic (read "moral") standards of postwar America. The bureaucratically enforced wholesomeness of American comic books (parodied unmercifully by their bastard offspring *Mad*) made the medium a specially circumscribed cultural space in which the terms of social rebellion were strictly defined: a comic book which violated the supposedly universal "standards of good taste" was simply not suffered to exist.[10] As a result, when America's rebelling youth of the 1960s set about breaching their culture's established taboos, the comics medium offered a particularly fruitful ground for iconoclasm. Besides the much-heralded innovations in popular music, the most influential and distinctive artistic achievements of the 1960s counterculture were the uninhibited and socially defiant underground comic books, which distinguished themselves from their Code-approved counterparts by adopting the soubriquet "comix." Underground comix were cheaply and independently published black-and-white comics which flourished in the late 1960s and early 1970s as outlets for the graphic fantasies and social protests of the youth counterculture.

To celebrate sex and drugs, as the counterculture did, was offensive to Middle America; to do it in the supposedly simon-pure comic-book form made the violation doubly piquant. The comix often paid homage to their comic-book ancestors by aping the unmistakable cover format and typography of the now-banned E.C. comics and by parodying the ubiquitous Seal of the Comics Code Authority; the interest of the comix in slaughtering sacred cows is clearly seen in the title of the long-running underground anthology *Dr. Wirtham's Comix and Stories*, which lampoons both anti-comic-book crusader Fredric Wertham and that hoary exemplar of good taste in comics *Walt Disney's Comics and Stories*.[11]

The comix creators cultivated an outlaw image, and their works systematically flung down and danced upon every American standard of good taste, artistic competence, political coherence, and sexual restraint; in so doing they created works in the sequential art medium of unparalleled vigor, virtuosity, and spontaneity—after the underground comix, the Comics Code would never be the same.[12] But comix were a short-lived phenomenon. By the middle 1970s unfavorable court decisions closed most of the drug paraphernalia shops ("head shops") which were the main retail distribution outlets for underground comix, the institution of "community standards" tests for obscenity restricted the areas where comix were allowed, and much of the counterculture's political and artistic energy had dissipated. Major comix artists still work in a format which may be called "underground," but surviving undergrounds retain only a shadow of their former vitality and transgressive force.

The underground comix were too idiosyncratic in approach and too multifarious in subject matter to be adequately summarized here.[13] In fact, their diversity was one of the revolutionary things about them, since they did not have to appeal to the widest possible audience, as did the Comics Code comics. They were a crucial phase in the development of sequential art as a means of artistic expression, and the underground comix movement of the late 1960s and 1970s formed the matrix from which emerged in the 1980s comic books that, unlike the iconoclastic comix, make a new and unprecedented bid for acceptance as literature. Jack Jackson was one of the earliest and most prolific contributors to the comix; Art Spiegelman began his career as a comic-book artist and editor in the undergrounds; Harvey Pekar's earliest work appeared in underground comix, and Pekar's most prominent collaborator on *American Splendor* is Robert Crumb, the greatest talent of the underground movement and one of the major figures in comic-book history.

The underground comix were the first significant group of comic books in America aimed at an entirely adult audience, and the comix proved to a whole generation of readers who had been raised on the vapid Code-approved comics that the sequential art medium is a powerful narrative form capable of enormous range and flexibility. The comix blazed the way for the present-day historical and autobiographical comic books by developing both a group of artists who could write fact-based narratives in comic-book form and an audience prepared to read them.

But while comics such as *American Splendor, Maus,* and *Comanche Moon* would not exist had there been no underground comix, they are not themselves undergrounds, and the difference lies in their attitude toward mainstream America; such writers as Jackson, Spiegelman, and Pekar now actively court a general reading audience. As the words "underground" and "counterculture" suggest, the comix set themselves up in opposition to the dominant culture of the 1960s and 1970s, and much of their energy comes from their persistent efforts to offend the sensibilities of bourgeois America. The comics of the 1950s, with their gory horror and crime extravaganzas, are as nothing, mere innocuous yarns of genteel taste and impeccable morality, compared with such underground classics as S. Clay Wilson's gross and hilarious "Captain Pissgums and His Pervert Pirates," Jim Osborne's tale of drug-induced murder and disembowelment, "Kid Kill!" from *Thrilling Murder Comics,* and Robert Crumb's nightmare/fantasy of castration in "The Adventures of R. Crumb Himself" from *Tales from the Leather Nun.*

Still, the adversarial stance of the undergrounds imposed its own limitations. Works of art which set out to offend most of the public are, if successful, reduced to preaching to the converted, and the unrestrained satire of the undergrounds did at times descend to sophomoric in-group smugness. Then too the thrill of breaking taboos palls with repetition as iconoclasm itself becomes a rote stylistic gesture. By the late 1970s what had been the underground comix movement was, like the counterculture at large, fragmented and dispersed in its energies. The characteristic psychedelic graphics of the comix had been coopted by American commercial designers; some of the less offensive satirists were absorbed into more respectable outlets for their work such as *Mad's* spiritual heir, the *National Lampoon*; and the end of America's involvement in the Vietnam War found the culture as a whole weary of the political and social confrontation on which the underground comix had thrived.

As a widespread cultural and artistic force the undergrounds lasted barely a decade. But their legacy continues, not only in the work of such established artists as R. Crumb, S. Clay Wilson, and Kim Deitch, who still create vital comic-book work, but also in a growing number of comic-book creators who take from the undergrounds new visions of possibility for comic-book narratives but without that antagonism toward a general audience which so often led to the self-ghettoization of the underground comix.

While all of the undergrounds made an implicit political statement in flaunting the Comics Code, many comix did and still do make overt political critiques of contemporary American society. Naturally enough, given the long tradition of comic books as a humorous form, the primary mode of ideological expression in the comix was satire, Juvenalian with a vengeance, and usually as salacious, scatological, and libelous as possible. For example, the cover of *Yellow Dog* no. 17 features a grinning, cigar-smoking devil, squatting hindquarters-on, defecating a suburban American landscape; in *Uncle Sam Takes LSD*, Uncle Sam similarly relieves himself of the head of Richard Nixon. Faced in their daily lives with the twin terrors of nuclear anxiety and the Vietnam War, the comix creators appropriated the horror genre to political and social satire.

Writers and artists such as Greg Irons, Tom Veitch, Dave Sheridan, William Stout, Rand Holmes, and Richard Corben used the conventions of horror comic books to satiric effect in comix that included *The Legion of Charlies*, which posits a military coup of the United States by the combined forces of Charlie Manson's murderous "family" and Lt. Calley's Charlie Company from the My Lai massacre. Politics and gore are inseparable in stories such as "You Got a Point There, Pop!" from *Deviant Slice Comix* no. 2, a tale of "the last war between men and women" featuring the black Amazon warrior "Ruth O'Leary of the fighting Fifty-first"; O'Leary informs her male captive that "the roots of the physical struggle between the sexes lies [sic] in the SEXISM and IDEOLOGICAL SUPREMISM of the masculine ego" just before she fries and eats his testicles.[14]

Among the longest running of the horror/satire anthologies were *Skull Comix* and *Slow Death Comix.*[15] *Skull* was not as overtly political as its more didactic and issue-oriented counterpart *Slow Death*, but the two comix shared many of the same contributors, and both took much of their tone and graphic format from the pre-Code E.C. horror comics. For example, advertising blurbs for *Skull* announced it as a comic "in the great old EC horror tradition," the front cover of *Skull* no. 1 sports an E.C. stamp ("An Exorpsychic Comic"), and on its inside cover the underground version of one of E.C.'s trademark "horror hosts," a grinning skull, welcomes his readers:

> Hi kids! Ever wonder what happened to those great old *HORROR* comix that used to scare the shit out of ya way back in the 50's? Well, they all disappeared, an' it wasn't *BLACK MAGIC* what done 'em in, either! Those comix are *GONE*! Until *NOW*, that is! Things bein' as they are these days, a few of us ol' characters decided it was time to revive th' *HORROR* comix… in keepin' with th' *times*, y'understand!… so here goes—Skull Comix gonna lay it on yer skull…. But ya better buy this *FAST* (or better yet, steal it)—cause ya never know when they'll have another great comic book cleanup![16]

Here the suppression of comic books by the Comics Code is implicitly equated with contemporary political oppression, "things bein' as they are these days," and the paranoia about "another great comic book cleanup" further connects the underground comix project to the unfettered comics of the early 1950s. The salutation "Hi, kids!" is clearly figurative, since the cover reads "ADULTS ONLY, KIDS!" The comix were hardly protective of tender sensibilities (R. Crumb was especially scathing about the American cult of childhood), but like most underground comix, *Skull* and *Slow Death* tried to protect themselves from confiscation and censorship by openly proclaiming their "adult" nature.

Slow Death too was inspired by E.C. comics, but its emphasis on environmental issues made the E.C. science fiction comics rather than the horror comics its natural forebears; *Slow Death* nos. 6 and 7 both mimicked the cover format of E.C.'s *Weird Science-Fantasy*, with its trademark rocket-ship sidebar.[17] For almost a decade *Slow Death* hammered away at the problems of overpopulation, environmental pollution, the extinction of animal species, and nuclear safety by means of stories which wed the conventions of science fiction and horror comics to social satire and didactic essays in sequential art form. For example, Greg Irons's "Our Friend Mr. Atom" in *Slow Death* no. 9 incorporates lists of facts about nuclear bombs and atomic energy in a discussion of geopolitics and cultural attitudes about nuclear arms; the story includes one panel in which a studio audience chuckles and applauds as a Johnny Carson–like talk-show host quips, "There are now enough atomic weapons to destroy the world 600 times over;" in another scene a Donald Duck–like Everyman figure has a huge atomic bomb hammered up his rectum.[18]

In some underground comix which used facts as part of their stories, the simple presentation of the horrifying data of pollution, corruption, and military insanity seemed to make the satiric point without using narrative at all. For example, Greg Irons's "Murder, Inc." from *Slow Death* no. 10 ("Special Cancer and Medical Issue"), includes a two-page spread which both embodies and comments upon the twin poles of sensationalism and didacticism characteristic of the use of facts in the undergrounds (and in historically based comic books in general). Most of the two pages are taken up by large blocks of closely spaced print, one headed "Fun Facts about the Medical Industrial Complex," the other entitled "More Fun Facts . . . The Doctors & the AMA." Across the top of both sections of print runs a comic strip in which a jackass and a baboon dressed as surgeons alternately butcher their comatose patient and attack each other over a botched drug deal. A rakish cigarette-smoking death's-head explains the relation between the two sections: "Now here at Last Gasp we realize that not all of you go for dry, informative, educational-type comic strips. All you sex and violence freaks can just SKIP the following fine print and groove on th' little cartoon here while the rest of you scholarly types read on." Here in "Murder, Inc." the uneasy solution of sober fact and brutal satire in the comix separates out into its component parts.

The educational impulse, with its implicit appeal to empirical authority, works against the visceral impact of the burlesque horror in the comix, which attacks authority by means of ruthless exaggeration and repulsive images. Satiric horror was an effective mode for recreating the anxiety and ugliness of modern industrial culture, but its penchant for shocking overstatement made it less effective in teaching about the particulars of a historical and political situation. Didactic and horror comix still exist, though now in separate venues. The present-day spiritual heirs to *Skull* and *Slow Death* are Kitchen Sink Press's *Death Rattle*, which published the work of horror stalwarts like William Stout and Rand Holmes, and the Educomics series, published by Leonard Rifas, which puts out informational comic books on topics such as nuclear power (*All-Atomic Comics, The Anti-Nuclear Handbook)* and corporate greed (*Corporate Crime Comics, Net Profit*).[19]

Besides their philosophical connections with the E.C. comics, the relevance of the now-defunct *Skull* and *Slow Death Comix* to the present discussion of true stories in the comics is that both comix were the most consistent underground sources for sequential art stories which combined the conventions of horror comics with factual data and history. They were likewise the principal outlets for the work of the artist whom one comics observer has called "the comics' foremost history teacher," the Texas-born Jack Jackson.[20]

1. The major exceptions were the Walt Disney line of comic books and the Gilberton Company's *Classics Illustrated* series; both publishers evidently decided that their products needed no outside certification of wholesomeness and did not subscribe to the Comics Code.

2. *Comics Code*, Preamble.

3. M. Thomas Inge, *Handbook of American Popular Literature* (New York: Greenwood Press, 1988), 79.

4. But the overtly juvenile genres still flourished: Carl Barks in *Donald Duck* and *Uncle Scrooge* and John Stanley in *Little Lulu* produced superb work unvexed by the social repression which throttled the adventure and horror genres.

5. Daniels, *Comix*, 86. For a fuller discussion of the history of the Comics Code, see Daniels's chapter, "The Comics Code Controversy," 83–90. Wertham himself favored a ratings system for comics rather than the thematic taboos of the Code.

6. *Comics Code*, part A, section 2.

7. A 1971 revision of the Code bows to humanity's persistent impulse to scare itself silly but only when ratified by tradition: "Vampires, ghouls and werewolves shall be permitted to be used when handled in the classic tradition such as Frankenstein, Dracula and other high calibre literary works written by Edgar Allen [*sic*] Poe, Saki (H. H. Munro), Conan Doyle and other respected authors whose works are read in schools throughout the world" (*Comics Code:* part B, section 5).

8. *Comics Code*, part B, section 2.

9. The Comics Code explicitly forbids the use of the words "terror," "horror," and "crime" in comic-book titles; among the most popular and controversial of pre-Code comics were E.C.'s *Vault of Horror* and *Crypt of Terror* and Lev Gleason's *Crime Does Not Pay*. Loss of sales soon forced Gleason out of business; E.C. had to cancel everything except *Mad. Comics Code*, part A, section 11; part B, section 1.

10. *Comics Code*, Preamble.

11. Dozens of comix used one element or another of the E.C. cover format. A typical comix use of the Code stamp appears on the cover of *New Paltz/Amazing Adult Fantasies* no. 2 (1974), where the stamp reads "Rated X Adults Only." For these and other examples, see Kennedy, *Comix Price Guide*.

12. The Comics Code was in fact revised in 1971 "to meet contemporary standards of conduct and morality," but the actual changes to the Code were minimal. Some mainstream comic-book publishers were heartened enough by this show of weakness to publish non-Code-approved stories dealing with drug addiction.

13. For fuller discussions of the history and social implications of underground comix, see Estren, *History of Underground Comics*; Kennedy, *Comix Price Guide*; and "Underground Comics" in Daniels, *Comix*, 165–193.

14. Both these examples are by Veitch and Irons.

15. Both published by Last Gasp Eco-Funnies, Berkeley, California. *Skull's* six issues (1970–1972) are a quite respectable run among the mostly one-shot undergrounds; *Slow Death's* ten issues (1970–1979) made it something of a comix institution.

16. *Skull Comix* no. 1 (San Francisco: Rip Off Press, 1970).

17. The cover of *Slow Death* no. 6 also included a facsimile of the Comics Code stamp being stuffed up a rectum.

18. *Slow Death* no. 9 (Berkeley, Calif.: Last Gasp, 1978).

19. For further information on Educomics, see Leonard Rifas, "The Origins of Educomics" in Kennedy, *Comix Price Guide*, 19–20, and "Leonard Rifas: Before It's Too Late," *Comics Journal* 92 (August 1984): 87–109.

20. Gary Groth in an interview with Jack Jackson, *Comics Journal* 100 (July 1985): 111.

3

From Violation to Education: Jaxon's Comic-Book Histories

Jack Jackson has earned his reputation as the best and most committed history writer in the comics. His comic-book histories include a stunning underground comix story, "'Nits Make Lice,'" two full-length biographies of figures from southwestern American history, *Comanche Moon*[1] and *Los Tejanos*,[2] and a narrative about Spanish Texas, "God's Bosom"; Jackson's recent horror/fantasy epic, "Bulto," uses extensive historical details of Spanish rule in the Southwest.[3] Jack Jackson published his earliest work in the undergrounds under the pseudonym "Jaxon" in order to preserve his day job with the state of Texas, and the pen name stuck throughout the 1960s and 1970s. Jackson began his career as a comics artist on the staff of a college humor magazine, the University of Texas *Ranger*; a collection of Jackson's strips from the *Ranger* period entitled *God Nose* (1964) is sometimes called the first of the underground comix.[4] In 1966 he moved to San Francisco where, along with several other expatriates from the Austin, Texas, area including the noted comix artist Gilbert Shelton, Jackson helped to establish in 1969 the underground comix publishing house Rip Off Press.[5]

While Jackson's initial style of drawing was much looser and more fluid in line than are his later, tightly rendered history comics, his interest in issues with strong ideological implications, especially the historical relations of American culture to minorities and Third World peoples, appears even in many of his earliest works. Jackson himself has disavowed a specifically political bent in his work, as he told an interviewer in 1982.

> JACKSON: I generally try not to get too political. I have no interest in being a political cartoonist at all.
>
> GROTH: Well the strip that I remember was very anti-bourgeois, very anti-establishment.
>
> JACKSON: Well, that's not political.
>
> GROTH: I thought so [laughter].
>
> JACKSON: No, that's not political at all. No, that's called survival of your brain, and mind, and so forth. Politics to me means something entirely different. I'm talking about your personal survival with your immediate environment. In terms of doing things like anti-development, anti-nuclear, anti-whatever. To me, that's entirely different than political. That's like the individual's duty. . . . if you decide that [something] stinks, then it's your obligation as an individual, a member of society, to raise hell about it. And that could be political, but it could also be highly personal. In other words, I wouldn't say, "Vote for Mr. So-and-So because he's going to change this" because maybe he will and maybe he won't. For a cartoonist or artist, this is a legitimate area to me, taking on big developers, or whatever happens to be going on around you. I don't consider it political.[6]

But "Vote for Mr. So-and-So" is not the only form of political discourse, and Jackson's distinction between "politics" (presumably meaning support for a specific candidate or law) and the individual's "survival of [the] brain" at first seems disingenuous, especially given the story in question. "White Man's Burden," from *Slow Death* no. 6, is a futuristic science fiction allegory depicting the final defeat of the now moribund white race by a coalition of what the narrator calls "the oppressed peoples—the black, brown, and yellow races." One of the Third World captors tells the last surviving young white male:

> Now, "boy," listen to the charges against you: You have enslaved your black brothers, stolen the red man's land, forced the Jews to be your shopkeepers, and the Orientals to wash your dirty laundry. You have poisoned the oceans, polluted the atmosphere, ravaged the land, wiped out the wildlife of the planet, reduced countless noble species to bones and dust and replaced them with new strains of vermin and disease.
>
> You have even debased *God* to your own image and contrived an *agonizing death* for his only son.[7]

"White Man's Burden" ends as the triumphant representatives of the Third World rush off in different directions to make a new world, each one, like the white man before him, secure in the belief that he has received a mission from God. Jackson himself has characterized the theme of the story as "in trying to destroy the oppressor we become just like him."[8] In no way can such stories, such rhetoric, be emptied of their political dimension: they *are* politics.

But Jackson himself defines the term more narrowly:

> "Politics" is not for me an all-encompassing element of human activities, certainly not to the extent of current usage. . . . [I] do not rank it high among the pursuits for which mankind was destined.
>
> My perception that most political endeavors are tainted by thinly disguised self-interest, involving the acquisition of material possessions or the exercise of power, makes the arena itself rather unsavory. Certainly "politics" is not a line of work for those seeking a greater understanding of man's proper place within nature's cycles and a reconciliation with the cosmic forces beyond our feeble mortality. . . . Politics, measured on such a scale, are rather petty and nonessential (even though the bastards can deprive us of our liberty and get us killed). When my work seems to reflect such themes it is usually because the impersonal maw of government has decided to devour yet another piece of our personal/interpersonal dimension.
>
> The way I see it, if Big Government—the insatiable feeding apparatus of "politics"—has the right to intrude into realms of consciousness where it does not belong, then surely I have the right to define what its proper role should be. Thus I do not consider myself a political cartoonist, especially not in the sense of a newspaper editorial cartoonist.[9]

Jackson's equation of politics with the oppression of governments reflects his lifelong sensitivity to social injustice, as his identification with the plights of Indians in *Comanche Moon* and Hispanics in *Los Tejanos* makes clear. While it can be argued that Jackson's attempt to educate America about its own history is itself a political gesture, Jackson firmly maintains that the task of the artist, "to reach an on-going state of self-awareness, to determine 'what it all means,' and then to convey these hard-won truths to our fellow creatures," is an endeavor in which political considerations are not primary but are "merely transient manifestations of a greater puzzle."[10]

This resistance of Jackson's to easy labeling of his work is characteristic and heartfelt. (He bridles at being called a "revisionist" historian, too.) Nevertheless, as histories and as comic books the works of Jack Jackson have strong cultural and ideological consequences. His comic books often show the struggle between the forces of established power and the socially disenfranchised. That such committed and passionate works in the sequential art medium have been created and published at all helps to indicate that there has been in the last two decades a significant change in cultural attitudes about comic books as a narrative form.

Jackson's two "graphic novels"[11] are full-length comic-book historical biographies of two nearly forgotten figures in American history: the half-white Comanche chieftain Quanah Parker (*Comanche Moon*, 1979) and the leader of those Mexicans who fought on the side of Texas independence in 1836, Juan N. Seguin (*Los Tejanos*, 1982). In scrupulous research and meticulous detail these comic books rival not only Harvey Kurtzman's E.C. war comics but traditional prose historiography as well. Kurtzman brought a new standard of accuracy and thematic sophistication to the already existing comic-book genre of thrilling war adventures; Jackson's achievement is to write narratives in the sequential art medium which introduce to the culture at large previously marginalized figures of American history.

The *Classics Illustrated* comic-book histories were intended as popularized adjuncts to formal scholastic education, and they attempt to lead their readers away from comic books to more respectable sources of information. Jackson's historical narratives, however, tell stories left out of the officially approved consensus versions of America's history. Together *Comanche Moon* and *Los Tejanos* help to uncover the buried history of America's rejection of the cultural "Other," the Indian and Spanish-Mexican races whose defeat was a part of the white Anglo victory in North America. Academic historians have not entirely ignored the Comanches and the Tejanos, as the bibliographies to Jackson's works make clear. But what historians say and what the culture thinks about itself can be two very different things. Comic books have long been one of the places where America shows itself what it looks like, and Jackson's historical comics thus comprise in their very narrative form an intervention in the process of cultural mythmaking.

The Past as Analogue to the Present: "'Nits Make Lice'"

The change in Jack Jackson's work from the underground comix to his more formal comic-book histories is not a change in his treatment of historical materials; all Jackson's historically based narratives share the same careful attention to detail and thoughtful use of historiographic scholarship which won praise for his *Los Mesteños*. It is instead a more conciliatory attitude toward the expectations and sensibilities of his audience. The difference between the underground comix and today's comic books aimed at an adult general readership can perhaps best be demonstrated by a consideration of one of the most powerful and shocking historical stories ever published in the underground comix. Jackson's "'Nits Make Lice,'" from *Slow Death* no. 7 ("Special Issue: True War Tales"), is a nine-page historical narrative about one of the worst military atrocities on the North American continent, the Sand Creek Massacre in 1864, where a regiment of Colorado militia attacked and wiped out a sleeping encampment of peaceful Cheyenne and Arapaho Indians, mostly women and children, in present-day Oklahoma.[12]

The Sand Creek Massacre was a crucial event in the story of the American frontier. The unprovoked attack helped to unite and solidify Indian resistance against accommodation with the whites, and the gruesomeness of the atrocities served to mobilize white reform groups in opposition to the government's Indian policy.[13] The influence of the Sand Creek attack was felt for decades in American domestic policy and in Indian distrust of the United States government, but the event has not entered the general cultural mythology as have such similar episodes as George Custer's disaster at the Little Bighorn in 1876 and Custer's massacre of Black Kettle's Cheyenne camp on the Washita River in 1868.[14]

Perhaps the Washita incident (and the tragic Wounded Knee coda to frontier history) has come to stand in our minds for all massacres of Indians by whites, just as the Little Bighorn fight has overshadowed similar historical events, such as the slaughter of Captain William Fetterman and eighty soldiers near Fort Phil Kearny in Nebraska in 1866. But the contemporary relevance of the Sand Creek Massacre comes not from the mere fact that soldiers killed Indians; American frontier history is full of bloodshed and atrocities on both sides. Through a narrative strategy which dramatizes the political context of the Colorado Territory in 1864, Jackson's "'Nits Make Lice'" implicitly connects America's past to its present. To tell in 1975 the story of Sand Creek, adhering always to the facts of received history, is also to conjure up the specter which haunts recent American history, that of Vietnam.

"'Nits Make Lice'" begins with a one-page prologue (figure 4) in which a sergeant recruiting for the Third Colorado militia regiment

Figure 4. Jack Jackson, "'Nits Make Lice,'" prologue
© Jack Jackson

makes his pitch to two ragged and bleary-eyed drunks in a Denver saloon. He appeals first to their bloodlust ("Say, how'd you boys like to kill a few Injuns?") and then to their greed and salaciousness: "..And.. we git to divy up th' LOOT!! Eh? Horses, mules, pelts, eh? And I hear some of them Cheyenne wimmen jest LOVES white stuff.. How bout that? Ever had any of thet Injun pussy, huh? HAW HAW"[15] The prologue establishes the soldiers at Sand Creek as ne'er-do-wells who are motivated by drink and the promise of plunder and rape.

Jackson's visual style is highly detailed, though the human figures are clearly caricatures; the soldiers and recruits are dirty, leering, and gap-toothed.[16] In fact, the image of the grinning soldier with missing teeth recurs at the height of the slaughter at Sand Creek; throughout "'Nits Make Lice'" the configurations of the people's mouths are an important cue for characterization. On the prologue page (six square panels in three tiers), the change in the faces of the central figures between the first and last panels demonstrates the process of brutalization which takes place in their recruitment: at first the expressions of the two drunks are blank, their mouths neutral as they sit at their barroom table, "seriously hung over," while in the last panel, one man sports a moronic grin, and the mouth of the other twists grotesquely, his missing teeth prominent in profile. Behind the gap-toothed recruiting sergeant, a pop-eyed gawker looks to join the fun. The visuals make clear that these Denver layabouts have been energized into ugly motion by the sergeant's base and repulsive appeal. The visuals also undercut the ostensible public reason for the campaign against the Indians.

In the first panel of the second tier the sergeant overcomes the drunkards' initial resistance to his come-on by playing up the idea of revenge for Indian depredations: "What's th' matter? Didn't you see those bodies we brought in yesterday? Innocent women and children, butchered like that? Don't it make you feel like doing something about it?!" The two reply: "I saw 'em.... Horrible ..." and "Murderin' redskins..." But the faces of the men, partially cut off by the panel borders, are dirty and gross, their expressions demonic. Their attempt at righteous indignation rings utterly hollow, and the charge of "innocent women and children, butchered" foreshadows the slaughter these men will later perform.

Jackson's dramatization of the enlistment of two Denver drunks puts a human face on history, the narrative equivalent of Harvey Kurtzman's trademark device of focusing on the story of a single individual in the midst of sweeping military campaigns. But where Kurtzman's stories nearly always suggest that each person is a helpless pawn swept along by an indifferent historical force, Jackson's story implies the opposite: historical forces themselves consist of the aggregate of individual human choices. Here hatred of Indians blends with lust and alchoholism to produce soldiers hired and trained for atrocity. Indian hating becomes a cultural locus for a whole complex of desires: sexual lust, both for the forbidden dark-skinned Other and in displaced form for the white "innocent women"; economic greed for loot from the Indians (and by extension the white men's greed for Indian land); and the urge to physical aggression, as the rest of the story makes agonizingly clear.

Like the splash page of Kurtzman's "First Shot," Jackson's title page is entirely without direct dialogue; only the narrator in the captions speaks. The visuals set the snowswept physical scene and establish the characters by means of close-ups of a freezing cavalryman swilling booze from a flask and of Chivington's grim stare. The page displays one of the characteristic moves of comic-book histories: here, as in the E.C. example, panels without dialogue coupled with a fact-heavy narrative voice work to exploit the temporal dialectic of sequential art in a way which is especially suited to historical narratives. Tellings of history require an interplay between the particular event and its general context, with each event highlighted enough for its importance to be clear and compelling yet appropriately subordinated to the overall schema of the historical narrative. In sequential art, the visuals give an immediate representation of a present-tense moment in time, while the narration can range over time, choosing the information which will establish the historical situation without overshadowing the event at hand.

The title page of the story switches from the dregs of the Denver saloons to the arrival of the Third Colorado regiment at Fort Lyon in November 1864 as the story moves closer in time and space to the catastrophe. The verbal narration introduces the commander of the militia force, Col. John M. Chivington; gives a short recap of the former preacher's Civil War service; and characterizes his motives for the events which are about to occur:

> Chivington! The man who, disdaining a "praying commission," blocked the way to the rebs in New Mexico and returned to Denver a conquering hero.

> A man who will stop at nothing to bolster his falling political stock, and as everybody in the Colorado Territory knows, there's no way to do that like KILLING INDIANS.

The narrator implicates the society as a whole in the events about to take place by showing that Chivington's attack on the Indians has been conjured up by the politics of the Colorado Territory. Chivington's attempted political revival follows a long American tradition of using Indian corpses as the stepping-stones to fame, and the splash page of "'Nits Make Lice'" establishes Chivington as both personally responsible for the massacre and part of a larger national syndrome of Indian killing.[17]

In "'Nits Make Lice'" the prologue and three following pages set at Fort Lyon give the explanation for the horrors shown in the last five pages set at Sand Creek. The Third Colorado militia regiment and its fanatical commander are not simply anomalous sadists, though at first Chivington's blood lust seems to be spurred by a vague sense of military machismo. When an army officer, Captain Silas Soule, objects to the pending attack on Black Kettle's peaceful Cheyenne, Chivington explodes in rage: "I say damn any man who sympathizes with redskins!! I've come here to KILL Indians, and by God, that's what I'm going to do! And you'll do the *same,* or face a court martial!" The obsequious commander of Fort Lyon, Maj. Scott J. Anthony, assures Chivington that the men of his command are "spoiling for a fight." Chivington then announces his intentions as the major provides a toadying counterpoint:

> Good! Good! That's what we're here for! I've got 600 men and their enlistments are up real soon. Till now, we're the laughingstock of the Territory—the "Bloodless 3rd" they call us. Well, not any more! We're gonna start wading in gore, right Major?
>
> We've got 'em in our fist, Col. All we have to do is SQUEEZE.

But if these words suggest that Chivington and his men intend to kill Indians simply to prove their manhood, the next panel shows the connection between Chivington's actions and the larger societal structure:

> A TOTAL VICTORY, that's what we need! HEADLINE MATERIAL! Ahem.. As you may know Major, Gov. Evans has tapped me to represent the territory in the capacity of Congressman. Now we've already got the miners and stockmen behind us. Statehood can't be far away.. A wagonload of scalps would just about clinch it at election time.
>
> That's wonderful, sir—just wonderful! Colorado needs your type of leadership.

Chivington's desire to kill Indians, any Indians, is a clear index of his suitability for leadership in Colorado Territory. Madman he may be (Captain Soule thinks to himself "My God . . . He's nuts. . . ."), but Chivington's racism and homicidal mania mesh smoothly with the political goals of his society. The interior views at Fort Lyon feature desks, pens, books, and the other trappings of the military bureaucracy, and Chivington delivers his bloodthirsty lines with his feet propped up on Major Anthony's desk, puffing a cigar in the iconic pose of the self-satisfied boss. In the white man's view of the world given here, Indian scalps translate directly into votes, and genocide is just good management.

Chivington relaxes as well in the last panels of the story. He sits in his headquarters tent after the successful attack on the Cheyenne and Arapaho encampment, once again lounging behind a desk and smoking a cigar. Between the frame formed by this recurring image are four pages, each with six panels, which show in graphic detail the butchery at Sand Creek. These four pages are among the most gruesome and horrifying ever presented in the underground comix, which makes their images among the most violent in any pictorial medium anywhere. The atrocity panels are worth the effort it takes to examine them closely, not only because they help to illuminate that attitudinal difference between the underground comix and more recent comic-book historical narratives which is under discussion here, but also because they raise important questions about the ethics of historical representation in visual media: can the truth be too awful to be seen? Is there an aesthetics of atrocity?

What "'Nits Make Lice'" does in sequential art simply could not be done in prose. For example, one major detailed account of the horrors of Sand Creek, Dee Brown's magnificent Indian history *Bury My Heart at Wounded Knee,* quotes at length, without editorial comment, the testimony of eyewitnesses before a congressional committee investigating the atrocity.[18] This calm recital of facts has its own peculiar power, since the reader must take the genteel euphemisms adopted by frontiersmen who are testifying before Congress and as it were "translate" them into the actions which the words signify and the attitudes such actions entail.[19]

The prose narrative is terrible enough. Chivington's unwilling scout, the half-Indian Robert Bent, told Congress: "I saw one squaw lying on the bank whose leg had been broken by a shell; a soldier came up to her with a drawn saber; she raised her arm to protect herself, when he struck, breaking her arm; she rolled over and raised her other arm, when he struck, breaking it, and then left her without killing her."[20] One of Jackson's panels (figure 5) shows, if not this specific scene, then one very like it: a barebreasted Indian woman with both her hands cut off lies on her back staring blankly at the bleeding stump of her right hand; her baby sits crying against her body as the stump of her left forearm sprays blood on the child's toy buffalo in the foreground; in the background a mounted soldier rides off after new victims waving a sword dripping with gore.

The point here is not to award the palm for horror to one medium or the other—the syntactic repetition of Bent's phrase "when he struck, breaking" is as sickening in its own way as Jackson's visual depiction of severed limbs. But the effect of each medium is different. The inescapably linear decoding of a sentence of prose allows the reader to assimilate its elements piece by piece, and the syntactic structure of the sentence provides a ready-made container for handling its meaning; threatening meanings are at once presented and kept at bay. Sequential art protects its reader too, though with different devices—the frame of the panel "contains" the narrative, and the conventions of pictorial representation constitute a grammar and syntax of visual cues. But the near-simultaneous apprehension of a picture is a more visceral and immediate physical act than the reading of prose.

In reading Robert Bent's steady recitation we can adjust our own impressions of what he means by the key words "struck" and "breaking" so as to arrive at an image which is not too disturbing for us. By the time we have perceived Jackson's picture, however, it has done its work. We must either look at it or physically turn away, and repulsion in narratives of atrocity is perhaps the most appropriate "reading" we can give. The underground ethos of "anything goes" allows Jackson to fling the decorum of academic histories to the winds; "'Nits Make Lice'" suggests that the horrific facts of the American past are too important to be veiled behind the indirect locutions of genteel historiographic prose.

A simple description of the panels of atrocity will indicate the depth of the horrors shown in "'Nits Make Lice.'" The ostensible leader of the expedition, Colonel Chivington, disappears from the narrative as the desires instilled in his men come to bloody fruition. In the sequences after the panel of the dismembered woman, soldiers shoot an old woman in the back. A man prepares to castrate a dead chief as he announces "I'm agonna' make me a tobacco pouch out of old White Antelope's go–nads." A young woman is gang-raped,

Figure 5. Jack Jackson, "'Nits Make Lice,'" page 7
© Jack Jackson
"This illustration demonstrates how the underground comix were
unflinchingly willing to depict man's inhumanity to man."—Jack Jackson

then her head is crushed by a rifle butt, in repulsive close-up. One gloating soldier holds up a woman's dismembered breast and says, "Got me a tit satchel," while another displays a bloody vagina and says, "How about this?! Fuzzy one, huh?" A naked and disemboweled pregnant woman crawls away, her fetus atop her protruding intestines. A beautiful young woman is scalped, and her hair makes a ghastly "pop" as the soldier pulls it free. And in perhaps the most emblematic image of military atrocity, four diabolically grinning soldiers hold an Indian baby aloft on their bayonets.

Jackson's pictorial representation in "'Nits Make Lice'" owes much to the visual style of horror established in the E.C. comics; Jackson has said of the influence of the E.C. horror comics, "How can you shake something like that?"[21] But the critiques of American society in the E.C.'s were oblique and implicit. For example, the E.C. "horror hosts" used punning references to corruption and putrefaction to mock America's obsession with hygienic commodities.[22] Here the exploitation of the conventions of horror comics in the context of a historical narrative takes this story beyond mocking satire into angry polemic. The usual grim humor of underground comix ultraviolence drops away along with traditional historiographic standards of "objectivity." To be an "unbiased" historian in the face of such atrocities as Sand Creek, this story implies, is to be less than human.

This story of an obscure frontier incident might seem like mere historical muckraking were it not that the images in "'Nits Make Lice'" were in 1975 achingly familiar to American audiences. The racially inspired hatred for the enemy, the brutal killing of women and children, the mutilation of the dead, the burning of villages, the "civilized" frustration with an elusive and hard-to-identify foe: all these aspects of the American West are likewise elements of the continuing American experience with nonwhite peoples which reached fruition in the war in Vietnam. American military commanders in the Vietnamese jungle ("Indian country"), and under a similar political pressure to produce body counts, would echo Colonel Chivington's words from a century earlier: "Whoever heard of peaceful Indians, huh? They're peaceful when it suits them and then they sneak out to murder, burn and pillage the unprotected citizens of this Territory!!"[23] Simply by inserting "Viet Cong" in place of "Indians" we see the essential continuity of American attitudes towards enemies. "'Nits Make Lice'" suggests that to suppress Sand Creek from our cultural memory ensures that it will return to haunt us.

The cover of the comic book which contains Jackson's story, *Slow Death* no. 7, satirically enforces the connection between "'Nits Make Lice'" and its present cultural situation. William Stout's cover drawing shows a blonde woman holding an infant running toward the viewer; in the background on each side of her stand lobsterlike bipedal aliens. The alien on the right is in the act of shooting the woman in the back with a futuristic raygun, and we see the blast emerge above her right breast, splattering the baby with her blood. The creature on the left holds a book titled "Rules" and looks distressed as it says, "Wait, Fon, *WAIT*!! The intergalactic code of war states that...," to which his fiercer comrade replies, "Don't worry, Tront! *GOD* is on *OUR* side!!"

The image on the cover echoes Jackson's panel of the Indian woman being shot in the back, though this time the woman is clearly contemporary, Caucasian, and middle class. She wears stylish boots, a "Keep on Truckin'" T-shirt, and a WIN ("Whip Inflation Now") button, details which place the scene securely in our own time: Gerald Ford's mid-1970s economic panaceas and R. Crumb's countercultural whimsy are both immaterial to the invading crustaceans. This satiric comment on those who would use law to separate war from its essential atrocity projects America's present into the future, just as "'Nits Make Lice'" shows the roots of the present in the past; science fiction and history are alike in using other times to show us who we are now.

To the Indians and to the Vietnamese the Americans were indeed alien invaders, mouthing pious ideals while in their frustration wreaking a destruction which fell most heavily on the weakest. "'Nits Make Lice'" gives the lie to America's conceit that its ideals as a culture preclude atrocities by its members, that any killings of innocents in its wars are isolated and unusual incidents. Jackson's historical narrative shows the My Lai massacre to be only the latest episode in an American tradition of interracial slaughter; "'Nits Make Lice'" implies that atrocity is not an anomaly but rather the habitual response of American racism.

Perhaps the most disturbing aspect of both William Stout's cover and "'Nits Make Lice'" is not the gore, which after all is a staple even of our movies for juveniles, but the graphically depicted violence against women: these pages conflate race hatred and gender hatred through the use of comic-book conventions. Both the cover and the story feature beautiful big-breasted women being killed; Jackson's pages make an explicit link between sexual aggression and murder, with close-up scenes of rape and genital mutilation. Stout's depiction of the fleeing woman, with her visible nipples and exaggerated breasts and pubis, partakes of the often overtly sexist conventions of underground comix representations of women; the uninhibited expression of the fears and desires of the mostly male underground artists entailed a good deal of sexism and misogyny.[24] In addition, the undergrounds were committed to breaking *all* taboos, including those of feminism; the comix artists saw the pressure to be "politically correct" in their works as a repressive left-wing form of the Comics Code. Like most comix artists, Jackson himself sometimes did erotic/pornographic stories; as he said in response to an interviewer's question about one of his sex stories ("Tales of the Leather Nun's Grandmother"), "Sure. It was a fuck story, and nothing's wrong with a fuck story in itself."[25]

But the images of the women in "'Nits Make Lice'" function differently from the drawings of naked women in so many underground comix, where they are often projections of libidic power or anxiety. Just as Jackson's narrative exploits our generic expectations of western adventure comics in order to draw readers into a story which has profound political and moral consequences, so too the images of women in "'Nits Make Lice'" enforce a relation between reader and text which implicates us in the story itself. Reading a comic book always entails a degree of Peeping Tomism, as we peer through the "windows" of the panel borders at a world beyond our own, and when this formal voyeurism is overlaid on the pictorial conventions of pornography to tell a historical story, readers become complicit in the action within the panels: the compositional breakdown in the gang-rape panel places the viewer literally within the circle of leering soldiers awaiting their turn at the victim.

"'Nits Make Lice'" disturbs in part because its form will not allow male readers, at least, the reassuring distance we seek from the horrifying attitudes it depicts. Even in their politically self-conscious underground incarnation, American comic books have been primarily the domain of "boys' stories," and the very notion of "atrocity" which fuels the justified outrage in these pages presupposes a male perspective on the world: the crimes by Chivington's men are specifically against women and children, and the most powerful images of the story show violations of motherhood itself. The massacre is made possible by the absence of the Indians' male power; above the picture of the baby spitted on bayonets, the narrator laments, "Sad day this, warriors of the Cheyenne, for you to be away, hunting the buffalo...." After the death of White Antelope and the loss of his patriarchal power, the narrator says, "Then the carnage begins ...," and one of the following panels shows White Antelope's castration. A moral center by which to judge the outrages comes in the form of the sympathetic army officer Captain Silas Soule, who, the narrator says, "powerless to stop the butchery, wander[s] about in a daze"; Captain Soule thinks "My God ... They're just women + kids...."

"'Nits Make Lice'" takes its title from Colonel Chivington's words in the final sequence of the story. As Chivington dreams of political glory, a sergeant appears at the door of the headquarters tent with a group of Indian women and children; he says, "Excuse me, sir, but Company C just brought in a batch of prisoners—." A demonic-looking Chivington replies, "PRISONERS???! Don't bother me with CRAP, Sgt. We're not taking prisoners—big or little. Don't you know that NITS MAKE LICE?"[26] The narrator continues in the last panel, "Vaguely annoyed at the stupidity of sergeants, Chivington returns to his report, totally oblivious to the screaming, abruptly silenced by a volley of shots." The story ends with a visual irony: a close-up of Chivington's hand shows him signing his battle report, with the words "All did nobly" highlighted on the page. Nobility is of course a strongly male concept, and it traditionally includes largesse in battle toward women, children, and others customarily bracketed out of the sphere of combat because of their supposed inherent weakness.

Though Jackson's story never mentions the historical sequel to the massacre, Chivington was rebuked by Congress, and his political hopes were dashed by public horror over the atrocities at Sand Creek. The deeper crime of Chivington and his men was to strip away the pretensions embodied in the rules of "civilized warfare" to reveal the naked aggression behind American Indian policy, which justified the displacement and domination of the Indians by asserting the superiority of white culture. But Sand Creek evoked the ultimate horror: the hated and exiled Other turns out to be oneself. The scolding congressional report on the "Massacre of Cheyenne Indians" makes the point explicitly: "Wearing the uniform of the United States, which should be the emblem of justice and humanity; ... having the honor of the government ... in his keeping, [Chivington] deliberately planned and executed a foul and dastardly massacre which would have disgraced the veriest savage among those who were the victims of his cruelty. . . . [He committed] acts which savages themselves would never premeditate."[27]

The structure of Jackson's story drives home the point that the white soldiers enacted the very crimes they accused the Indians of committing: Chivington was unable to appease the blood lust of his society and to present it with a pleasing image of itself, one which did not reflect back the savagery and rapine of its Manifest Destiny. "'Nits Make Lice'" is by nature of its presentation and its place in time a powerful indictment of American imperialism, and its images of racism and misogyny implicitly compare the 1864 massacre to present horrors in the United States and in Vietnam; gender and race become the ways in which America knows its victims.

Graphic depictions of real-life horrors like "'Nits Make Lice'" could be published only in the underground comix; a version of the Sand Creek massacre approved by the Comics Code, if such a thing can be imagined, would of necessity disguise the nature of the events. Jackson's story takes the freedom from traditional standards of "decency" which the underground artists appropriated to themselves and uses it to force a confrontation with the American past; the story turns the reader's repulsion to political account. A pictorial narrative of atrocity engages its viewers in a way that prose simply cannot do, and the question becomes whether a truthful account of historical horror can be both accurate and decorous. As we shall see below, Art Spiegelman's story of the Jewish Holocaust, *Maus*, poses the same question in a slightly different way.

"'Nits Make Lice'" is arguably the most harrowing historical story ever published in the bloody milieu of the underground comix, and its power is indisputable. But to force readers to undergo a moral and visceral ordeal in order to read a comic-book story naturally limits one's potential readership. Women especially are likely to be alienated from reading stories like "'Nits Make Lice,'" since the very fact of the gender-linked violence can overshadow the seriousness of its representation. The Sand Creek story is a watershed in Jack Jackson's career. "'Nits Make Lice'" does more than simply astonish the bourgeoisie; even readers who were sympathetic to its political viewpoint were horrified at its shocking presentation of atrocity and its bleak and despairing vision of history.

Jackson saw the need to be more considerate of his readers' sensibilities and more patient with their expectations if his work were to be effective in teaching Americans about their own history. After

"'Nits Make Lice'" Jackson's comic books become even more committed to historical accuracy, and the stories he chooses to tell continue to bear important cultural consequences, but Jackson's historical epics, *Comanche Moon* and *Los Tejanos*, adapt the scrupulous integrity and adult perspective of the underground comix in order to tell histories which go beyond the small circle of underground comix readers to reach a general reading audience.

True Western Adventures: Comanche Moon

In the late 1970s Jack Jackson published a remarkable trilogy of comic books which depict the story of the Texas Comanche leader Quanah Parker: *White Comanche* (1977), *Red Raider* (1977), and *Blood on the Moon* (1978).[28] A revised and expanded version of Parker's biography was published in trade paperback form as *Comanche Moon* (1978). While most historical stories in comic books have of necessity been short and episodic, *Comanche Moon* is a full-length history, complete with maps, archival photographs, and a bibliography of prose sources. In *Comanche Moon* Quanah Parker's story is a microcosm for the history of his Indian society. As a fierce war chief, Quanah led the Comanches against the whites in the last years of the Plains Indian wars; as an Indian statesman after the final defeat of the Comanches, he both helped to promote coexistence between the Indians and their white neighbors and fought to preserve traditional Indian culture against white encroachment.

Parker's life thus encompasses the entire historical process of the Indians' displacement in America. Jackson's history covers familiar ground in an unfamiliar way. The facts of Quanah Parker's life have been told many times but primarily in the form of prose histories; Indians have long been grist for the comic-book mills but almost always as savage redskins or noble savages. But *Comanche Moon* is neither an indictment of white greed nor of red barbarity, though the narrative shows incidents of Anglo venality and Indian brutality. Its documentary visual style resembles the detailed panels of "'Nits Make Lice,'" but *Comanche Moon* replaces the atrocity story's aggressive rage with a more restrained tone and an evenhanded attribution of historical responsibility.

Jackson himself saw his approach to his audience in *Comanche Moon* as a departure from his previous work in the underground comix. For example, the story includes a swimming-hole scene between the young Quanah and a "Comanche maiden." Jackson's treatment of nudity in the original comic book version is typical of the underground comix: the sequence features the young woman's large and rather pneumatic breasts. In the graphic novel *Comanche Moon*, the panels have been redrawn and the figures repositioned so that the woman's flowing hair covers her breasts. An interviewer, Bill Sherman, asked Jackson, "What prompted this act of self-censorship?"

> JACKSON: That strip I did in *Slow Death*, "'Nits Make Lice'" [7]. It's a very depressing and frustrating comic strip, and the reaction I got from European readers and a lot of American readers, too—well, they were horrified by it. After I started getting some feedback on that strip, it got me to thinking that you really have to decide how you're going to treat your reader with that kind of strip. How far are you going to go: are you going to work completely for yourself, risk estranging yourself from your reader, or are you going to try to reach *them*? What's the point: to satisfy your own whims or reach the most people? Like with the rape scene in the first Quanah Parker book. I could've focused on it.
> SHERMAN: Like you did in "'Nits Make Lice.'"
> JACKSON: Right. But the reaction I got to those scenes made me realize they weren't appropriate in the Parker books. I treated the scene through the eyes of the children instead of focusing on it per se. Now I realize that was the most effective way to do it.[29]

No artist works "completely for [him or herself]," of course; any artistic creation implies *some* audience. For the underground audience, which was already alienated from mainstream American culture, the "estrangement" that Jackson mentions was a positive value; often the weirder and more repulsive a comix artist could be, the better. To move beyond that audience, or to find a new one when the countercultural readership dissolved, required an accommodation to conventional artistic standards, as Jackson's comments imply.[30]

A high price was paid for mass audience appeal. The uninhibited sex, violence, and vulgarity in the comix showed America the kinds of freedom of expression that had been swallowed up in the tyranny of "redeeming social value"; the excesses of the underground comix were culturally valuable precisely because they were gratuitous. In the underground comix, comic-book artists who were limited only by their artistic skill and depth of imagination produced stunning works which expanded the boundaries of the sequential art medium forever. That Jack Jackson, one of the most iconoclastic of the comix artists, felt compelled to "self-censorship" in his works indicates how the comix artists came to see that even full freedom can become an artistic dead end.[31]

The central move of the underground comix creators was to ignore entirely the repressive and artificial rules of decorum imposed on comic books by the Comics Code Authority and on artistic expression in general by bourgeois standards of "good taste." Jackson's realization that the rape scenes so vital to the impact of "'Nits Make Lice'" were not "appropriate in the Parker books" reinserts into adult comix the concept of artistic decorum, the matching of style to content; says Jackson, "you have to ask the question of what the story demands."[32] But now what is considered "decorous" for a comic book has been radically redefined by the formal and imaginative gains made by the undergrounds.

Jackson's revisionist history in *Comanche Moon* faces a double bind. The underground audience (or its remnants) which is most familiar with both Jackson's work and the characteristic gestures of the comix is likewise a group that is suspicious of history in general; the counterculture was more comfortable with smashing icons than with reshaping them. But general readers with an interest in Indian history could very well be put off by the comic-book form of the narrative itself, let alone the more flamboyant visual grace notes (nudity, graphic violence) which are part of *Comanche Moon*'s considerable underground comix inheritance. Jackson's historical works appeal to both audiences by wedding the careful research and gripping narrative drive of Harvey Kurtzman's E.C. war comics to the political and formal self-awareness of the undergrounds.

Comanche Moon is "revisionist" history precisely because of its narrative form. Jackson picks no bones with prose historians of Quanah Parker's life and introduces no new startling facts. As he says in the credits to *Comanche Moon*, "There is nothing new in this book. The story has been told by many other writers, to whom I am deeply indebted. I have only sifted their work, placing emphasis on events according to my limited grasp of the rapidly shifting historical panorama."[33] The "placing of emphasis [on] events" by giving an Indian's-eye view of Texas history in *comic-book* form constitutes the originality of *Comanche Moon*.

Jackson's Quanah Parker is a new kind of comic-book Indian. Though the image of the snarling, bestial redskin is perhaps the most familiar one to comic-book readers, Indians have sometimes been treated without hostility in comic books about the American

West.[34] This generally condescending sympathy takes several forms. Sometimes the Indian is seen as being essentially similar to white men, though endowed with special kinds of knowledge because of his barbaric origin; in this version he becomes a white man's side-kick, like the Lone Ranger's Tonto. Another image is that of the fierce primitive doomed by his untamable wild Otherness to extinction in the face of civilization, like the warrior chiefs Sitting Bull and Crazy Horse. But Quanah Parker's half-Indian, half-white heritage gives Jackson the opportunity to combine and transcend these clichés; Quanah is neither a noble lackey, nor a white man in red-face, nor an inscrutable barbarian king.[35] *Comanche Moon* insists on Quanah's humanity and his importance as a historical figure, a man "who embodied the best qualities of both races."[36]

The first section of the story, titled in its comic-book form *White Comanche*, shows the capture of Cynthia Ann Parker as a child, her upbringing as an Indian (with an Indian name, "Naduah"), her marriage to the Comanche chief Peta Nocona, and the birth of their first son, Quanah. Cynthia's indoctrination into Indian ways allows Jackson to make the details of Comanche life familiar to the reader before Quanah enters the stage. Some elements of Indian culture do resemble white ways of doing things, like the recreational visits to "resort areas" enjoyed by the Comanches,[37] while many others (eating dogs, for example) obviously do not. Jackson's approach to his material in *Comanche Moon* allows us neither a too-easy familiarity with the life of Quanah Parker nor a reassuring distance from it. The final effect is that we get to know a man as well as if he were our friend while being reminded in his every action that we made him into our enemy.

One of the primary techniques by which Jackson accomplishes this dialectic of familiarity and distance is through the use of dialogue; the characters in Jackson's histories speak in an extraordinary blend of archaic and contemporary diction. Jackson's Indians use a variety of styles, ranging from the stereotypical grunts and "Hows" of stage Indians to the most formal kinds of oratory, depending on the context. Among themselves in informal situations (and especially in unspoken thoughts) the Comanches speak an easy and colloquial form of standard English. For example, when the young Quanah joins a friendly band of Comanches after his father's death, the chief of the group welcomes him formally: "Your father was a bold and courageous man, a true QUOHADA. Stay with us...," while a sympathetic onlooker thinks to himself "But watch yourself, kid."[38]

In another panel General William Sherman and some United States troops arrest the Kiowa chief Satanta, who had bragged about a raid on a wagon train; Sherman says, "It's the end of the rope for you guys!" and the distressed chief thinks, "Me and my big mouth!"[39] Jackson's dedication to *Comanche Moon* indicates a source for this narrative technique: "This book is dedicated to Jack Patton and John Rosenfield, Jr. and their little comic book 'Texas History Movies,' which taught generations of Texas schoolchildren more about the history of our state than they SHOULD HAVE KNOWN, and to the kids of tomorrow, whose delicate minds will mercifully be spared the shocking truth about their ancestors."[40]

In an article on Patton and Rosenfield's *Texas History Movies*, Jackson quotes an early introduction to this Texas-produced educational comic, and the quotation applies equally well to all of Jackson's own history comics: "Effort has been to make the figures of Texas history living, vital, human figures and not stilted personages. In order that the humanness of the story can be presented, the pictures and text material are at all times colloquial and idiomatic."[41]

Attaining the proper balance between words and pictures is one of the perennial problems of sequential art, and Patton and Rosenfield's technique of colloquial diction gives Jackson's history comics an amazing verbal range and stylistic versatility. We have seen how Harvey Kurtzman's E.C. page used words and sound effects as crucial design elements, but the compositional role of words in comics is not only a technique to be exploited at will. The placement of words and dialogue on the page is one of the inescapable problematics of sequential art narration, and in the creator's rush to present information in a history comic the words can get out of hand. Comic pages which attempt to present a great deal of verbiage in a limited space can deteriorate into panel after panel of talking heads intoning blocks of exposition at one another. In the superhero comics this is not often a serious problem, since the rudimentary conflicts mandated by the Comics Code can usually be represented well enough visually.

In other genres, especially educational comics in general and historical comics in particular, the didactic impulse threatens to overwhelm with words the visual impact which makes sequential art such an effective narrative medium in the first place. The narrative of *Comanche Moon* covers almost a hundred years and includes a wide range of topics: the personal history of Quanah Parker and his family, the political and other power relations within the Indian bands, Indian relations with the whites, and elements of the political, social, and economic history of Texas. Some parts of the story, like the depictions of Texas geography, Comanche life, and the various battles, lend themselves well to pictorial representation. Other, very necessary aspects of the narrative, such as specific historical data like names and dates, as well as the interior thoughts and emotions of the characters, rely solely or primarily on words. Jackson's varying dictions help keep his comic from getting too text heavy and his characters from seeming like the usual "stilted personages" of prose historiography.

In *Comanche Moon* Jack Jackson uses two entwined strands of verbal narration. In the caption boxes which accompany nearly every panel, a formal and precise narrative voice supplies historical background in the present tense and makes transitions from scene to scene. The caption boxes themselves are sometimes drawn to resemble pieces of parchment with frayed ends, or they can be scrolled across two panels, linking the narrative in each panel and lending a note of solemnity to the narrative voice, as did the caption boxes in the *Classics Illustrated* panels discussed in chapter 1. Within each panel the characters generally speak as if they were modern Americans, with a few blatant anachronisms. For example, as Quanah elopes with another man's fiancée, one bemused watcher says, "I can't wait to see the look on ol' Tennap's face," and another replies, "Boy, is he gonna be bent out of shape!"[42]

The exceptions to the modern diction almost always have an ideological point: Indian and white public oratory uses the conventions of formal speech, and situations in which whites condescend to Indians or Indians ingratiate themselves with whites use the stereotyped diction of Hollywood Westerns. These various levels of diction work continually to subvert our generic expectations. When, overjoyed at the release of his family from army captivity, an Indian chief tells a cavalry officer, "Bull Bear thanks Three-Fingers 'Kenzie. You heap good pony soldier—*like Comanche!*" Bull Bear's broken English is familiar to us from dozens of popular portrayals of Indians in the movies and on television; in fact, the phrase "heap good" is cultural shorthand for "Indian talk." When, however, on the very next page, the governor of Texas says to some chieftains newly freed from prison, "Just remember—the first time you mess up, it's back to the joint!" the genre switches to something closer to the gangster movies of the 1930s.[43] Sometimes the clash of dictions takes place within the panel; in one instance (Figure 6) a guard taunts the imprisoned Satanta in mocking pidgin, "Hey Chief! What's the matter—no likee makee chairs?? Hahahaha," while Satanta thinks in modern

Figure 6. Jack Jackson, *Comanche Moon*, page 76
© Jack Jackson

colloquial English, "I'll go nuts if I don't get outta here...."[44] Satanta's response highlights the cultural gulf between the men; the Indian's speech is closer to our own than is the white man's.

Jackson's dialogue calls attention to itself because it is unlike the stilted and heroic diction usually found in comic books, but his pictures are usually restrained, with a documentary, almost photographic attention to physical details.[45] The visual style makes the truth claim of realism; it suggests that this is what the past would look like if we were there. When the photographic-seeming pictures are combined with the modern-sounding words of the characters, the overall stylistic strategy of *Comanche Moon* creates a world that looks and sounds familiar to us. At the same time Jackson's work denies us the familiarity of genre; we cannot read Quanah Parker's life as simply another cowboys-and-Indians story. Neither does its verbal style supply us with the distanced voices of traditional historiography, where quotations from documents and historical accounts serve to remind us that the happenings of the narrative took place long ago and far away from our own cultural situation. Jackson's comics take advantage of the immediacy available in sequential art narratives to attempt the recreation of history as the actions of "living, vital human figures" whose world, though past in time, is finally continuous with our own.

The physical format of *Comanche Moon* itself affects the kinds of narrative strategies available to Jackson. The traditional page length of commercial comic books limits the ways they can tell historical stories; at about thirty-two pages, most comics do well to present the particulars of a single incident. But at 129 pages *Comanche Moon* is long enough to give its subject full-length treatment. The sweeping events of the late nineteenth-century Texas Indian wars still require a good deal of narrative compression, but in the available space Jackson can at least suggest important connections between one incident and another.

Comic-book histories have traditionally approached their narratives as a series of discrete episodes; even the 100-page *Classics Illustrated* special issues such as *The War Between the States* and the Gilberton Company's *World Around Us* series consisted of separate stories, sometimes linked by illustrated prose passages, and even the best of the *Classics* stories ruthlessly cut out exposition and detail. *Comanche Moon* uses the figure of Quanah Parker to give focus to its history of the Texas Comanches and thus presents each of its incidents as part of a single historical story. *Comanche*

Moon contains much more explanatory material than most comic books with a historical theme; at only ten pages even a top-notch history comic such as Harvey Kurtzman's "Custer's Last Stand"[46] does a much better job of presenting thrilling historical circumstances than of explaining why they are important to the nation's history.

The episodic approach to history in most commercial comics is no doubt a convenience for producing comics on a deadline, but it also has a deeper philosophical consequence. As mentioned in the discussion of the title page to "'Nits Make Lice,'" one of the central problems facing historical storytellers is how to supply the appropriate amount of background information to explain the significance of the story without diluting the immediate impact of the particular event. History comics often sidestep the problem entirely. Comic-book writers can simply exploit history as a source for sensational adventures, making the historical context irrelevant. Jackson drew attention to the difference between the two poles of historical storytelling in an interview:

> GROTH: Do you find it difficult to reconcile those two aims—to entertain and to instruct?
>
> JACKSON: Well, it is in the case where you're working with a story that's basically tragic. If it's a lighthearted sort of thing, like Davy Crockett fighting bears, well, of course you can get away with a lot of stuff that you don't have to go into whenever it's more educational. It's kind of hard to balance it, really.[47]

Jackson's two graphic novels demonstrate his willingness to "go into" whatever is necessary to tell his stories in the detail he deems appropriate. Key incidents, especially those which lend themselves to visual presentation, do receive multipanel treatment. But much of *Comanche Moon*'s story is told in single-panel snippets which supply the political, cultural, and social context of the specific episodes. For example, Jackson devotes three pages comprising thirteen panels to various occurrences throughout Texas in 1858–1860, including a government attack on Buffalo Hump's Comanche village, Comanche raids into Mexico and the resulting Indian trade with renegade Mexican Comancheros, the worsening relations between white Texans and the reservation Indians, the breakup of the Texas reservation system, and Peta Nocona's stepped-up raids against white frontier settlements. In this sequence Jackson generally shows each scene in one or at most two panels.[48] This information helps to show why the next event happens; immediately following this quick-moving overview, Jackson uses the same amount of narrative space (three pages, thirteen panels) to show Cynthia Ann Parker's recapture by white men at the Pease River in 1860, a single event which covers only a few hours.[49] Even though *Comanche Moon* was originally published as three separate comic books, and additional material amounting to yet another comic was added for the collected version, the smooth integration of historical context with specific events makes Jackson's graphic novel an apparently seamless telling of a single story.

Comanche Moon, unlike Jackson's later and more overtly educational *Los Tejanos*, was written primarily as a result of Jackson's personal interest in a story familiar to Texans; Jackson says that in the Parker story "the idea [was] to entertain."[50] Jackson is able to subvert our generic expectations so effectively because those expectations are in place to begin with; as Jackson says, "Everybody's got their general fantasies about the way life was on the plains with the Indians."[51] But *Comanche Moon*'s story has strong ideological implications nonetheless.

Quanah Parker is not exactly a tragic hero, and *Comanche Moon* does not cast him simply as a victim of white expansionism. Though his people were defeated and he was sometimes called upon to fight and kill his own white relatives, he ended his long life respected by both whites and Indians, and his strength and wisdom helped the Comanches make the difficult transition from their traditional wild freedom to their new life under white civilization. Parker's mixed blood represents a model of mutual assimilation between the white and Indian cultures, one which was rejected in the white Anglo conquest of North America. Parker is a figure who blends two antagonistic cultures which never rationally resolved the conflict between the rights of the Indians and the desires of the whites. By choosing such a transitional figure as his subject, and by telling his story in comic-book form, Jack Jackson reshapes the popular notion of the western frontier.

Comanche Moon implicitly encapsulates in Quanah Parker a vision of American history in which the Indians are not simply bestial threats and obstacles to white progress or nature-loving martyrs to white imperialism. The Indians in *Comanche Moon* instead are members of a complex culture whose sometimes violent interaction with our own has made America what it is. Jackson's history shows us that, whether we are white or red, Quanah Parker is a part of us.

The Lost History of Texas: *Los Tejanos*

Jackson's next project picks up the theme of the person caught between two cultures, but *Los Tejanos* tackles a historical subject which is much more troublesome and problematic than that of *Comanche Moon*. Quanah Parker, while not as familiar to the general American public as more widely celebrated Indians such as Crazy Horse or Geronimo, is still famous enough in western history, and his eventful and adventurous life is well documented. In *Comanche Moon* the notion that "history" can be presented transparently, without ideological intrusion or historical bias, is relatively easy to sustain. Historians generally agree about the facts of Quanah Parker's life, and the defeat of the Indians by white culture, while still a subject of discussion, is essentially a dead issue for the culture at large. But *Los Tejanos* tells the story of a highly controversial figure, Juan Nepomuceno Seguin, a leader in the war for Texas independence who was eventually driven to fight for Mexico against his former Texas allies; Seguin is thus considered a traitor by both Texas and Mexico.

The historical disputes about Seguin and his life raise issues which are central to the establishment of the Texas Republic and to the history of Anglo-Hispanic relations on America's southwestern border; millions of Hispanic Americans in the Southwest find themselves in a cultural situation parallel to that of Juan Seguin. As a result, *Los Tejanos* as a work is much more self-conscious in its narrative than is *Comanche Moon*, much more aware that it presents a story which present-day Americans need to know.

The Seguin story first appeared in comic-book form as *Recuerden El Alamo* (1979) and *Tejano Exile* (1980), both published by Last Gasp. Where *White Comanche*, the first comic-book segment of *Comanche Moon*, begins with a short homage to the prose historians of the Texas Comanches, *Recuerden El Alamo* starts with Jackson's own introduction to the story of Juan Seguin, and the bibliography to the larger collection, *Los Tejanos*, bemoans the lack of a modern history of Seguin.[52] Jackson makes clear that *Los Tejanos* is not a simple rearrangement of unproblematic facts, as he maintained in *Comanche Moon*, but instead a passionately felt reconsideration of popular notions about the Texas Revolution. Jackson writes:

> When we "Remember the Alamo," it is usually a vision of a small, grim band of Anglo-Saxon martyrs being overwhelmed by a screaming horde

of maniacal Mexicans, their bayonets glistening with the blood of patriots as they trample in endless waves into the sanctuary of Texas liberty.

What we don't remember is that *inside* the walls of the Alamo, among its defenders, there were also Mexicans who fought and died, except they called themselves "Tejanos"—Texans! Nor do we remember that at the battle of San Jacinto, where in eighteen minutes the fate of a vast land was decided, there was also a company of Tejano volunteers fighting beside Sam Houston and the Anglo conquerors. . . .

This book is an attempt to pay homage to these brave souls by following the true story of one such man, Juan Nepomuceno Seguin, an early revolutionary leader among the Mexicans of Texas. Had he been Anglo, his name would be remembered among the lists of the great—beside Travis, Crockett, Bowie, and the rest. But being Tejano, his contribution has been ignored, for his exploits did not conveniently fit into the myth of Anglo-Saxon prowess that historians have seen fit to fashion from the events of our revolution (and that films like John Wayne's version of "The Alamo" have since perpetuated).[53]

Los Tejanos thus attempts to reshape the way American culture views its history. More specifically, as the phrase *"our* revolution"[54] suggests, *Los Tejanos* is aimed at least partly at a local Texas audience for whom the events at the Alamo and San Jacinto have a personal significance. People take their history seriously in Texas, as Jackson explained to an interviewer:

> It got so I had to watch how I was describing *everything* in [*Los Tejanos*]. A lot of these people have descendants in this state, so I can't just say, for instance, that Sam Maverick ripped Juan off. I have to back off or describe it as an allegation. Because you can really piss somebody off. I'll tell you: just last week I got an anonymous phone call. I picked up the receiver and there's this voice, choked with rage, saying, "You asshole. If I ever get the chance, I'm gonna cut your fingers off."[55]

Since early Texas history still raises emotions in this way, Jackson cannot simply reinsert Seguin into the pantheon of frontier heroes. Even in his own time people told conflicting stories about Juan Seguin, and in retelling Seguin's life Jackson must pick his way through a minefield of historical obscurity and contemporary animosity. The story of Juan Seguin and the Texas-Mexicans is an exceptionally complicated one, comprising as it does the history of prerevolutionary Texas and Mexico, the 1836 war itself, the Byzantine political maneuverings of the fledgling Texas republic, and its eventual annexation by the United States. The course of Seguin's life is simultaneously the process by which he and his Tejano people have been written out of history; Seguin's story undoes in its very telling part of the injustice that Jackson argues was done to the man and his memory. The erasure of Seguin from Texas history was a literal one; Jackson's introduction to the second comic-book installment of the Seguin saga, *Tejano Exile,* says:

> Events which took place in Texas after the revolution have made—and continue to make—Juan Seguin one of the most controversial characters in Texas history. So controversial that the page from the original minutes of the town of Seguin—naming it in his honor—is ripped from the book, bearing mute testimony to the label "traitor" that Juan Seguin has borne for over a century.[56]

Jackson's comic book attempts to force a reconsideration of Juan Seguin. The introductions and bibliographic notes with which Jackson frames his books stress that Seguin's life has important consequences for present-day Anglo-Hispanic relations: "To understand contemporary events in the Mexican-American sphere, one must have a knowledge of men like Juan Seguin, his problems, and his fate in an Anglo-dominated society."[57]

The present discussion cannot hope to deal with all the narrative, historiographic, and cultural issues raised by a complex and unusual work like *Los Tejanos.* But the specific effects of Jackson's chosen narrative medium do deserve attention here. That is, how does the comic book form of the work function to create a historical narrative? More than any other comic-book creator, Jack Jackson works in the narrative traditions of prose historiography, and *Los Tejanos* clearly shows some of the problems and opportunities that arise when history is told in comic-book form.

The vast number of characters and incidents and the knottiness of the conflicts in *Los Tejanos* make its structure much more complicated than that of the fairly straightforward *Comanche Moon.* While Quanah Parker's story incorporates a great deal of historical information, its major outlines can be traced in a series of visually impressive scenes: the capture of Cynthia Ann Parker, Quanah's extravagant vision quest, the various raids and battles between the whites and the Comanches. But in *Los Tejanos* the battles are only illusory watersheds; the troubles of the Tejanos begin *after* the Texas revolution has been fought and won, and the downfall of Juan Seguin is a slow shifting of public favor and personal loyalties, not a catastrophe in battle. As a result, in covering its information *Los Te-*

janos is exceedingly text heavy, and very few incidents are told in more than one or two panels.

To avoid the pictorial claustrophobia induced by pages of small panels with large blocks of text, Jackson uses in *Los Tejanos*, as he did in *Comanche Moon*, a three-tier page layout (figure 7) which often features single long horizontal panels as one tier; almost never does Jackson use the full six panels possible in his "three-deep" layout. For pages of the most visually striking action Jackson uses three long panels to a page, one panel per tier, giving an "open" feel to the narrative which is highly appropriate to its setting on the plains of Texas. But most often the single panels appear above or below tiers of two panels each, a layout which allows more space for incidents which will move the narrative along.

Some of the narrative effects which Jackson achieves with this layout are possible only in sequential art. For example, we saw in the *Classics Illustrated* Fort Sumter pages how images from one panel can suggest subliminal connections to later ones (as when the Union gun appeared to fire the Confederate shot), but in *Los Tejanos* the immediacy of the comic-book page is exploited more fully and more subtly. An example of exceptionally effective layout manipulation occurs in *Tejano Exile*. Jackson explains in two pages the complicated process by which, after the battle of San Jacinto and Texas independence, marauding Anglo cattle stealers with quasi-official license, bands of Tejano cattle bandits, and the long-established legitimate Tejano cattle ranchers ultimately clash in a series of range wars. Jackson's two-page spread integrates six separate panels into a single overall composition which shows visually the conflict that words can only describe.

At the top of the left-hand page is a single-panel overhead shot of a frontier town, deserted because of war, which has been converted into a holding pen for stolen cattle. Below this long panel are two smaller panels which explain the widening scope of the cattle rustling and the helplessness of the authorities to prevent it. On the facing right-hand page, another long panel shows the holdup of a Mexican trading party by Tejano *bandidos*. Below the panel of the bandidos is a long panel of Tejano ranchers responding to news of a cattle raid, and the layout and its accompanying text make it unclear whether the raiders are Mexican or Texan, an ambiguity which fits the complex conflict perfectly. The layout physically connects the two groups of robbers by placing the panel showing the spoils of the Anglo rustlers directly across from one which depicts the Tejano bandits in action.

Figure 7. Jack Jackson, *Los Tejanos,* pages 58–59
© Jack Jackson

This linking of related images is a common and effective storytelling technique, but the best effect on this two-page spread is even more evocative. Below the panels which explain the events on the Anglo side, a group of cowboys rides to the attack; under the scenes of the bandidos and the honest ranchers, a band of *rancheros* defends itself against the advancing Anglos. This panel thus becomes the final panel for both pages; verbally bringing the action to a climax is its caption, "To survive, the rancheros must fight fire with fire. Soon all the area of 'West' Texas is aflame with terrorism."[58]

The page gutter functions as a fluid panel border; as we read to the end of the right-hand page, the panel seems to be cut off, but as we get to the bottom of the right-hand page, we perceive that each section of the picture is part of a larger panel. Since the panel is shared between the pages, we must return to the left-hand page after we have read the right. It takes much longer to describe the layout in prose than it does to perceive its effect on the page. By imaging the conflict between the rustlers and the ranchers in a single emblematic picture rather than by showing specific incidents, Jackson concisely presents a complex historical process in a way only comic books can do.

Jackson later exploits the emblematic potential of sequential art to show another, even more intricate political situation (figure 8). During the American Civil War, some Tejanos joined the Confederate Texans, others supported the Union, and the conflict within Mexico between pro-French Imperialists and Mexican Juarez Liberals split Tejano and Anglo loyalties even further; all this information is needed to explain Juan Seguin's career as a pro-Juarez soldier and his role in the Mexican victory at Puebla on May 5, 1862. The problem is how to present this tangled situation without having the narrative bog down in long explanations. One of Jackson's solutions is to give a panel in which representatives of various groups address the reader and state directly how they feel. The caption reads, "The situation in Mexico is complicated by the conflict between the *French invaders* and the *Juarez liberals*, who are backed by the Union."[59]

In the panel two Confederate officers link arms with a gaudily dressed Hispanic as they face the reader, as if posed for a snapshot. One Confederate says, "Like most Confederates, I favor the Imperialists." The other tells us, "I'm a Reb, but I still like Juarez. . . ." The grinning Hispanic confides, "I like who pays th' most!" Even if we know little about Civil War politics in the Southwest, these attitudes make sense. The pro-Imperialist Confederate enunciates the

Figure 8. Jack Jackson, *Los Tejanos,* page 121
© Jack Jackson

traditional Texan hatred of the Mexican government, and he echoes a Tejano Confederate two panels earlier who says, "Us aristocrats have to stick together!"[60] The second officer connects the Confederate rebellion against the Union with the Juaristas' revolt against the French. The mercenary third man (Tejano? Mexican?) shows just how fluid the loyalties can be, with so many different groups having so many reasons for sympathy with or antipathy to one another.

The symbolic concision of this panel suggests an illustration for an elementary school history textbook, an appropriate connection, given Jackson's frequent assertion that he was inspired by the comic book/textbook *Texas History Movies* and given his avowed didactic purpose in *Comanche Moon* and *Los Tejanos.* Jackson has said of his historical comic books, "I'm a big believer in the teaching value of these things,"[61] and his work displays a new synthesis of entertainment and education in comic-book form. Some of Jackson's panels are composed with the formality of nineteenth-century historical paintings, as when Seguin joins the Juaristas and when he fights at the battle of Puebla;[62] others make jokes of historical anachronisms, as when a newly prosperous Tejano cotton farmer strolls through a blizzard of wind-blown bolls singing, "I'm dreaming of a white Christmas. . . ."[63]

Los Tejanos performs a didactic function by calling attention to the previously disregarded existence of Juan Seguin and the Tejanos, and in trying to teach readers about history in comic-book form, it resembles the *Classics Illustrated* comics. But where the *Classics* attempted to wean their readers away from comic books, Jackson's histories encapsulate in their textual form a new stance toward mainstream history. An alternative writing of American history demands an alternative narrative medium, and the suppressed stories of minority figures such as Quanah Parker and Juan Seguin find an appropriate home in the culturally marginalized form of comic books.

Jackson gives full bibliographies to his works and invites his readers to discover prose histories of the Comanches and the Tejanos. But as the erasure of Juan Seguin's name from civic records tells us, documentary records and historical narratives can obscure as much truth about the past as they reveal. Histories can indeed tell falsehoods, but the greater danger is that their truths will be accepted as the whole story, and that their ideological assumptions will go unnoticed and unquestioned. An important part of what Jackson teaches his readers in *Los Tejanos* is that history itself is not simply the open book of the past but rather a story which requires continual interpretation and thoughtful reexamination.

The historical comic books of Jack Jackson represent a contemporary extension of both the sober didacticism of the *Classics Illustrated* histories and the gritty realism of Harvey Kurtzman's E.C. war stories. Jackson gives his historical narratives an ideological complexity far beyond that of the straightforward, socially approved history versions of the *Classics*. Where the Gilberton comics helped to indoctrinate its young readers into the values of bourgeois America, comic books such as *Comanche Moon* and *Los Tejanos* force us to consider the human and cultural price that was paid for the triumph of those values. Harvey Kurtzman's careful research into historical background and period physical details in *Frontline Combat* and *Two-Fisted Tales* resulted in sophisticated and uncompromising war stories, but the comics failed economically because, in the mid-1950s, an adult comic-book audience had not yet developed. Jack Jackson's histories, while accessible in form and in vocabulary to young readers, exploit the thematic and stylistic gains of the underground comix to create narratives which aim at expanding both the historical consciousness of contemporary American culture and the bounds of what is possible in the sequential art medium.

1. Jack Jackson, *Comanche Moon* (San Francisco: Rip Off Press/Last Gasp, 1979).
2. Jack Jackson, *Los Tejanos* (Stamford, Conn.: Fantagraphics Books, 1982).
3. Less well known to comic-book readers is Jackson's monumental illustrated prose history of cattle ranching in Spanish Texas, *Los Mesteños* (College Station: Texas A&M University Press, 1986), as well as other historical works such as his collection of Indian portraits, *Long Shadows: Indian Leaders Standing in the Path of Manifest Destiny, 1600–1900* (Amarillo: Paramount, 1985), and, with Maurine T. Wilson, his *Philip Nolan and Texas* (Waco: Texian Press, 1988).
4. See, for example, Jay Lynch, "The First Amendment Was Easier Then," in Kennedy, *Comix Price Guide*, 16–18.
5. See "Rip Off Press: The Publishing Company That's a Little like the Weather," *Comics Journal* 92 (August 1984):69–83.
6. Jack Jackson, "Jack Jackson on His Work in the Underground and His New Book *Los Tejanos*," interview with Gary Groth (10 June 1982), *Comics Journal* 75 (September 1982):76.
7. Jack Jackson, "White Man's Burden," *Slow Death* no. 6 (Berkeley: Last Gasp, 1974).
8. Jack Jackson, "Tejano Cartoonist," interview with Bill Sherman (28 August 1981), *Comics Journal* 61 (Winter 1981):102.
9. Jack Jackson to the author, 31 May 1988.
10. Ibid.

11. "Graphic novel" is the term currently in vogue for hard- and softbound collections of several standard-sized comic books; the term in England is "album."

12. For a bibliography on the history and historiography of the Sand Creek Massacre, see Francis P. Prucha, *American Indian Policy in Crisis* (Norman: University of Oklahoma Press, 1976), 11, n.20.

13. See ibid., pp. 11ff.

14. For a cultural analysis of the Custer's Last Stand mythos, see Richard Slotkin, *The Fatal Environment: The Myth of the Frontier in the Age of Industrialization, 1800–1890* (Middletown, Conn.: Wesleyan University Press, 1985). The Washita battle figures prominently in Thomas Berger's novel *Little Big Man* and in Arthur Penn's popular film version (1970).

15. The diction in Jackson's histories will be discussed more fully below, but it is worth noting here that the characters speak in a mixture of western dialect and contemporary phrasing, further strengthening the connections between the past and the present.

16. The stylistic mixture of detailed military accoutrements and slightly caricatured human figures was a trademark of the work of John Severin and Will Elder in the E.C. war comics; Jackson's style of rendering in his historical works is heavily influenced by Severin's work.

17. For further explication of American attitudes about Indians, see Richard Slotkin, *Regeneration through Violence: The Mythology of the American Frontier, 1600–1860* (Middletown, Conn.: Wesleyan University Press, 1973); and Richard Drinnon, *Facing West: The Metaphysics of Indian-Hating and Empire-Building* (New York: New American Library, 1980).

18. Dee Brown, *Bury My Heart at Wounded Knee* (New York: Simon and Schuster, 1981), 87–91. Jackson has indicated that Brown's narrative was a "catalyst" for "'Nits Make Lice'" (Jack Jackson, telephone interview, 23 May 1988).

19. For the full text of the congressional testimony and related documents, see *The Sand Creek Massacre: A Documentary History*, intro. John M. Carroll (New York: Sol Lewis, 1973).

20. U.S. Congress, 38th Congress, House of Representatives, second session, *Massacre of Cheyenne Indians*, appendix, p. 96.

21. Gary Groth in an interview with Jack Jackson, *Comics Journal* 100 (July 1985):111.

22. In "Till Death," from *Vault of Horror* no. 28 (December 1952–January 1953), the protagonist Steve's wife Donna returns from the dead as a zombie; the Vault Keeper says "I guess Donna *DONNA KNOW* about LIFEBUOY! But now that Steve's a zombie, at least she has a *DEADBUOY!*" This story is discussed in Daniels, *Comix*, 64–65.

23. For discussions of the connections between American frontier history and Vietnam, see Drinnon, *Facing West*, chapters 27ff.; and Slotkin, *Fatal Environment*.

24. The best underground comix presentation of the issue of sexism and artistic freedom is Robert Crumb's "And Now, A Word to You Feminist Women," in *Big Ass Comix* no. 1. See also Estren, *Underground Comics*, 114–139.

25. Jack Jackson, "Tejano Cartoonist," 109.

26. The "nits/lice" metaphor is discussed in Drinnon, *Facing West*, 502.

27. U.S. Congress, House Report, *Massacre of Cheyenne Indians*, v.

28. The trilogy was originally to consist of Cynthia Ann Parker's story, *White Comanche*; Quanah's life as a free Indian, *Blood on the Moon*; and the story of the Comanches after their defeat by the soldiers, *Whiteman's Road*. The material from *Whiteman's Road* along with several new pages and redrawn panels was incorporated into the collected *Comanche Moon*.

29. Jackson, "Tejano Cartoonist," 109.

30. Jackson did not bow to every cavil about his work. Some librarians objected to

the scene in *Comanche Moon* where the newly recaptured Cynthia Parker slashes her breasts in grief at the loss of her family. Whereas the nudity in the swimming scene was secondary, the self-mutilation scene is an integral part of the story, and Jackson did not change it.

31. Jackson himself sees the relation of artist to audience as only a "contributing factor" to the new directions chosen by some comix artists. He says, "The big reason is that certain artists were bored with repeating themselves and wanted to do something a little more intellectually fulfilling. Marketing was always an afterthought" (Jack Jackson to the author, 22 June 1988).

32. Jackson, "Tejano Cartoonist," 109.

33. *Comanche Moon*, 118.

34. Maurice Horn, *Comics of the American West* (South Hackensack, N.J.: Stoeger Publishing, 1977), 187. But Horn's assertion that "it is fair to say that the red man has always gotten a better deal in the comics than in the movies" is true more as an indictment of cinematic racism than as a paean to comic-book liberalism. For a typically racist view of Indians, see such comic books as *The Savage Raids of Chief Geronimo* (New York: Avon Periodicals, 1951).

35. The historical facts of Parker's life allow Jackson to sidestep the "half-breed torn between two worlds" cliché as well; Quanah Parker fought and eventually made his peace with white culture always as an Indian.

36. *Comanche Moon*, rear cover.

37. Ibid., 15.

38. Ibid., 43.

39. Ibid., 75.

40. Ibid., 2.

41. Jack Jackson, "Learning Texas History," *Comics Journal* 119 (January 1988):97. Jackson has credited *Texas History Movies* with sparking his own interest in telling historical stories in comic-book form (Jackson, interview, *Comics Journal* 100, p. 113).

42. *Comanche Moon*, 58.

43. Ibid., 80, 81.

44. Ibid., 76.

45. The figures in several panels are clearly modeled on photographs reproduced in *Comanche Moon*. See, for example, the splash panel of the recaptured Cynthia Ann Parker at *Comanche Moon*, 39. Jackson also acknowledges his debt to western artists such as Charles Russell and Fredric Remington (Jack Jackson, "Jaxon," interview with Bruce Sweeney, *Comics Interview* no. 9 [March 1984]:44).

46. *Two-Fisted Tales* no. 27 (May–June 1957).

47. Jackson, interview, *Comics Journal* 100, p. 113.

48. *Comanche Moon*, 33–35.

49. Ibid., 36–38.

50. Jackson, interview, *Comics Journal* 100, p. 113.

51. Jackson, "Tejano Cartoonist," 110.

52. *Los Tejanos*, 126.

53. *Recuerden El Alamo*, 2.

54. My emphasis.

55. Jackson, "Tejano Cartoonist," 110–111.

56. *Tejano Exile*, 2.

57. Ibid.

58. *Los Tejanos*, 58.

59. Ibid., 121.

60. Ibid., 120.

61. Jack Jackson, telephone interview, 23 May 1988.

62. *Los Tejanos*, 121.

63. Ibid.

4

History and Talking Animals: Art Spiegelman's *Maus*

The clearest sign that something unusual was afoot in the 1980s in the sequential art medium came in 1987, when the National Book Critics Circle nominated a comic book by Art Spiegelman for its annual award in biography.[1] Comic-book readers had long known of the work of Spiegelman, first as an artist, writer, and editor in the underground comix, and later as the coeditor of the avant-garde comics and graphics anthology *Raw*. But few people were prepared for the public acclaim for Spiegelman or for the media attention on the comic-book medium which accompanied the 1986 publication in book form of Spiegelman's *Maus: A Survivor's Tale*.[2] *Maus* garnered hundreds of reviews, almost all of them favorable, some wildly so, and the book quickly drew worldwide attention as "the Holocaust comic."

In *Maus*, a comic-book artist named Art Spiegelman tells the story of his father, Vladek, a Polish Jew who, with Art's mother, Anja, survived the Nazi concentration camp at Auschwitz. Taking his epigraph from Adolf Hitler, "The Jews are undoubtedly a race, but they are not human," Spiegelman draws the characters in *Maus* as anthropomorphized animals; mice are Jews, cats are Nazis, pigs are Gentile Poles, and so on. *Maus* tells only half of Vladek Spiegelman's story; the book ends with the arrival of Vladek and his wife at Auschwitz in 1944.[3] Though Spiegelman's project is as yet unfinished, the unprecedented critical reception for *Maus* has changed, perhaps forever, the cultural perception of what a comic book can be and what can be accomplished by creators who take seriously the sequential art medium.

If Jack Jackson's Texas histories raise controversial social and political issues, *Maus* leaps foursquare into "the most difficult ethical problem of the 20th century."[4] Serious literature in comic-book form is a relatively recent and slightly unsettling concept in American culture, but a comic book which takes on the Holocaust as a subject compounds the problem of artistic decorum a hundredfold. One powerful school of thought on the Holocaust denies the very possibility of any ethically responsible representation of the Nazi attempt to exterminate the Jews. The concentration camp survivor Elie Wiesel puts the case most forcefully: "There is no such thing as a literature of the Holocaust, nor can there be."[5] T. W. Adorno echoes Wiesel: "To write poetry after Auschwitz is barbaric."[6] In this view, to aestheticize in any way the profound evil of the Holocaust is to appropriate for one's own ends the unique experience of the victims of the gas chambers. In a society which views comic books as *essentially* trivial, *Maus* thus might appear as a grotesque degradation of the Holocaust, mocking the catastrophic sufferings of millions of human beings as the squirming of cartoon rodents.

But to acknowledge the insufficiency of art in the face of the abyss of human evil poses its own paradox. The imperative need for humanity to remember the Holocaust demands that the events in Europe before and during World War II somehow be turned into language. Are our ethical responsibilities to the victims of the Nazis and to posterity mutually exclusive? We must ask, "How does a 'respectful silence,' one that fully recognizes the mystery, the passion, the awesome uniqueness of the Holocaust, differ from the silence of neglect. Silence is silence—nothing more, nothing less—and it is silence that may, finally, be the unforgivable crime of those who could have spoken, but who did not, of those who could have joined the post-Holocaust debate, but were afraid."[7]

The arguments of those who oppose literary representations of the Holocaust cannot be brushed aside easily. Perhaps it *is* the case that to assimilate the Holocaust into our usual structures of thought, to pretend to "understand" the unthinkable, is a move that accepts the attempted genocide of European Jewry as one event among many in history, one which raises the possibility that the horror might happen again. Yet the Holocaust will not simply go away; its legacy is always with us, in the death camp survivors and their families and in contemporary international politics. If silence about the Holocaust is too problematic an option to embrace, the question then becomes one of authority and authenticity. Who has the right to speak? And when does the gap between art and life become so wide that fiction becomes a blasphemous lie? These are heady questions indeed to pose to a comic book, and it is a mark of Art Spiegelman's skill and courage as an artist/writer that *Maus* confronts and at least partially answers them.

Spiegelman's authority to speak on the Holocaust stems from a personal psychological necessity. In *Maus*, a frame tale around Vladek's biography shows in a series of present-day vignettes the mouse-narrator Art's difficult relationship with his crotchety and often insensitive father.[8] Though *Maus* was nominated for the Book Critics Circle Award in biography, it is perhaps more precisely an autobiography. In order to live his own life, Art must understand his relations with his parents. To do so, he must confront the Holocaust and the way in which it affected Vladek and Anja.

In the framing episodes, the mouse cartoonist Art visits Vladek to collect his father's memories for the book which will become *Maus*; he asks questions about the details of the story and tries to understand the implications of what Vladek tells him. The connection that Art and Vladek achieve in the telling and writing of the Holocaust story is continually undercut by their awkward and frustrating encounters in their everyday lives. The ostensible subject of the book, the Holocaust, is finally subordinated to the relationship between Art and Vladek as they collaborate on turning Vladek's memories into art. *Maus* is thus in large part about the process of its own writing.

This self-reflexivity and the psychological need to which it points are especially evident in the story "Prisoner on the Hell Planet: A Case History" (figure 9), a comic book embedded in the larger narrative of *Maus*. "Prisoner on the Hell Planet" is a four-page depiction from Art's point of view of the nightmarish events surrounding Anja's suicide in 1968; Spiegelman published the story in an underground comic book, *Short Order Comix* no. 1 (1973). In *Maus*, the story appears when a friend of Vladek's second wife, Mala, also a death camp survivor, sends a copy of the comic to the Spiegelmans. The presence of this story in *Maus* is perhaps Spiegelman's boldest and most brilliant stroke; it breaks the narrative flow of the Holocaust story and explains the emotional stake Art has in understand-

Figure 9. Art Spiegelman, "Prisoner on the Hell Planet," page 4
© Art Spiegelman

ing his parents' lives. The characters in "Prisoner on the Hell Planet" are humans; the story even reproduces a photograph of Art and Anja on vacation in 1958. The disruption of the animal motif passes without comment in *Maus;* never are the characters aware that we see them as mice.

Throughout *Maus,* Spiegelman's drawings are spare and almost primitive, with a minimum of line and only sketchily rendered details in the panels. But "Prisoner on the Hell Planet" is drawn with white lines on black scratchboard in a sophisticated and highly textured style that recalls German Expressionist woodcuts. The discrepancy in the way the two narratives look emphasizes Art's role in shaping his father's story. The plain, understated visual style depicting Vladek's Holocaust narrative matches the old man's flat and unemotional tone, just as the claustrophobic compositions and grotesquely exaggerated perspectives in the comix story approximate Art's overwrought mental state at the time of his mother's death. "Prisoner on the Hell Planet" shows that Spiegelman's visual style is a narrative choice, as constitutive of meaning as the words of the story.

"Prisoner on the Hell Planet" is a surreal first-person narrative casting Art as a prisoner of the guilt and paranoia inherited from his loving but emotionally oppressive parents. Art wears the striped pajamas of a concentration camp inmate, and the story implicitly connects his psychological suffering with his parents' ordeal in the Nazi camps. At the start of the story, just after he reports the fact of his mother's suicide, Art sets the emotional scene: "I was living with my parents, as I agreed to do on my release from the state mental hospital 3 months before."[9] At the end, the last three panels pull away, leaving Art in a metaphorical prison cell of grief and guilt. He addresses his dead mother,

> *Congratulations!* ... You've committed the perfect crime....
>
> ... *You* put me here.... Shorted all my circuits ... Cut my nerve endings ... And crossed my wires!....
>
> ... You *murdered* me, Mommy, and you left me here to take the rap!!!

Spiegelman undercuts Art's hysterical self-dramatization by giving the last word to another inmate, who says, "Pipe down, Mac! Some of us are trying to sleep!"[10] Only in "Prisoner on the Hell Planet" do we discover Art's motivation for gathering his father's story. Art cannot afford a silence about the Holocaust—respectful or otherwise.

He must confront the Holocaust in order to come to terms with the qualities in his father which made his own life so oppressive and guilt-ridden: the miserliness, the domestic tyranny, the personal insensitivity. *Maus* offers no sentimental apotheosis between father and son; each episode shows that the two men grow closer as Vladek recounts the past, only to have the familiar tensions arise once more when the anecdotes are over. Spiegelman has said of the cathartic function of writing and drawing *Maus:*

> In order to draw *Maus*, it's necessary for me to reenact every single gesture, as well as every single location present in these flashbacks. The mouse cartoonist has to do that with his mouse parents. And the result is, for the parts of my story—of my father's story—that are just on tape or on transcripts, I have an overall idea and eventually I can fish it out of my head. But the parts that are in the book are now in neat little boxes. I know what happened by having assimilated it that fully. And that's part of my reason for this project, in fact.[11]

By submitting his parents' experience to artistic form, Spiegelman attempts to control the legacy of the Nazi crimes in his own life. This therapeutic psychological process may well be seen as a distortion of history, and to put the Holocaust into "neat little boxes" may be a doomed effort to control the uncontrollable, as writers like Elie Wiesel suggest. Yet "Prisoner on the Hell Planet" shows the alternative. As his stay in the mental hospital indicates, Art has already been psychically damaged by the Holocaust; to fail to assimilate its consequences into his present life would be to ensure that the Nazis continue to torture Jews a generation after the fall of the Third Reich.

Like the problem of authority, the question of authenticity in fictional representations of the Holocaust appears overtly in *Maus*. Historical accuracy is important to Art. He consistently tries to persuade Vladek to supply the physical and emotional details which will set the scene and make clear the chronology of the complicated process by which the Nazis classified, segregated, and eventually moved to exterminate the Jews of Poland. But in historical narratives emotional truth is as important as period detail; a history must be both factually accurate and convincing as a truth-telling. While Art must draw out from his father the minutiae of the Final Solution, Vladek needs no urging to be honest about himself. Vladek is bluntly candid about the things he did to survive—the smuggling, bribery, black-marketeering, and string-pulling that helped him to keep himself and his wife alive while millions around them were dying.

In *Maus* Spiegelman never sentimentalizes Vladek's survival, nor does he gloss over the personal difficulties he has with his father. A more conventionally sympathetic view of Vladek would dilute the complexity of one of the most fully realized characters in American comic books. Spiegelman told an interviewer, "One of the things that was important to me in *Maus* was to make it all true,"[12] and despite the stylization of human beings as mice and cats, *Maus* makes good on the central tasks facing historical narratives—it is both convincing as a recreation of a past time and gripping in the story it tells.

Art Spiegelman maintains that the stylization of *Maus* is the very thing that enables him to write an authentic Holocaust narrative at all. He told an interviewer:

> If one draws this kind of stuff with people, it comes out wrong. And the way it comes out wrong is, first of all, I've never lived through anything like that—knock on whatever is around to knock on—and it would be counterfeit to try to pretend that the drawings are representations of something that's actually happening. I don't know what a German looked like who was in a specific small town doing a specific thing. My notions are born of a few score of photographs and a couple of movies. I'm bound to do something inauthentic.
>
> Also I'm afraid that if I did it with people, it would be very corny. It would come out as some kind of odd plea for sympathy or "Remember the Six Million," and that wasn't my point exactly, either. To use these ciphers, the cats and mice, is actually a way to allow you past the cipher at the people who are experiencing it. So it's really a much more direct way of dealing with the material.[13]

The subject matter of the Holocaust makes an enormous and immediate claim on the sympathies of an audience. In addition, the specific details of the extermination process are terrifying enough, yet perhaps more intolerable than the sight of mounds of rotting corpses is the realization that human beings are capable of creating them. As a result, in viewing representations of the Holocaust, audiences tend to slide with some relief into stock, often sentimental, responses rather than confront the threatening material anew. Spiegelman addressed the problem when he told an interviewer, "It's one of the banes of so-called Holocaust literature that when you're reading it you hear violins in the background, and a soft, mournful chorus sobbing."[14] By depicting the Jews and Nazis as animal figures Spiegelman can defamiliarize his too well known story and can sidestep the "already told" quality of the Holocaust. He escapes as well the overdetermination of meaning that the use of human characters would entail. The minimal lines with which Spiegelman delineates his characters permit a wide range of expression and gesture without too closely approaching existing human facial types.

The thematic role of the primitive drawing style in *Maus* becomes especially evident when we compare the full-length epic to Spiegelman's first attempt to work the Holocaust material, a three-page story entitled "Maus," first published in an underground comix title, *Funny Aminals* [sic] no. 1, in 1972.[15] "Maus" introduces some of the basic premises of the longer work—the animal metaphor, the frame device of the old Jew telling of his life to his son—as well as some of the same anecdotes, most notably the betrayal of Jews hiding in an attic.[16] But "Maus" also has some false notes which show how completely Spiegelman reworked his artistic approach when he set out on the longer project. For instance the mouse-narrator is named "Mickey," a one-shot joke whose Disney parody adds nothing to the Holocaust narrative. Later, the persecuted mice find shelter in a factory that manufactures kitty litter; again the humorous overtones of the detail work against the seriousness of the story itself.

Maus too is humorous at times, but the comedy is grimmer and more sharply focused on the historical situation, as when a scheming Jewish collaborator, a "kombinator," sells bootleg cake in the ghetto, only to find that he has put laundry soap into the batter instead of flour.[17] The animal metaphor is much more thoroughly applied in "Maus" than in *Maus* (the mice are small enough to hide under bags of kitty litter, for example). In the shorter version Spiegelman was able to tell the story without referring to Jews and Nazis at all (the oppressors of the mice are simply "die Katzen"), but such indirection was awkward and artificial in the full-length telling of the Holocaust story. Spiegelman's move away from stressing the animalness of his characters indicates how the genre of *Maus* likewise moves away from the animal fable toward a much more original application of the funny animal genre to history.

In "Maus" the faces of the characters, both mice and cats, are highly detailed and individual. Heavy shading and fully mobile mouths allow a wide range of near-human expressions, and the large, sad eyes of the mice make an especially strong pull on the reader's sympathy. The hooded, black-rimmed eyes and pointed fangs of the cats, in contrast, preclude any reader identification with them. The physical scale in "Maus" nearly approximates the natural relation of mice and cats; the Nazis tower over the much smaller Jews. The stylistic gestures of Spiegelman's first try at his father's story amount to overstatement, as the artist was the first to realize. When he set out on the full-length *Maus* project, Spiegelman considered a number of different drawing styles, including one using scratchboard. An example of this experiment (figure 10) was reprinted in an interview with Spiegelman; it is a cross between the expressionist woodcut style of "Prisoner on the Hell Planet" and the highly detailed cartoon style of the shorter "Maus." Spiegelman rejected this sophisticated visual style in favor of a more direct and immediate one which simply polishes his initial penciled breakdown sketches.

Spiegelman spoke of his efforts to match an appropriate illustrative style to the Holocaust material and explained:

> One solution I thought was interesting involved using this Eastern European children's book wood engraving style that I'd seen in some books of illustrations. But I found myself thoroughly dissatisfied with these woodcut illustrations after a day or so. My problems with the drawing are, I would hope, obvious. First of all, it banalizes the information by giving too much information and giving too much wrong information. It becomes like a political cartoon. . . . The cat, as seen by a mouse, is big, brutal, almost twice the size of the mouse creatures, who are all drawn as these pathetic furry little creatures. It tells you how to feel, it tells you how to think, in a way that I would rather not push.[18]

The subject of the Holocaust carries its own built-in value judgments and to a certain extent renders a work impervious to criticism; as Spiegelman's wife and co-editor of *Raw*, Françoise Mouly, said, "When he's doing a story on this subject matter, nobody's going to criticize and say, 'Yeah, they should have killed all the Jews!' The subject already has a certain sacred element to it, and the scratchboard drawing reinforces this."[19]

Spiegelman finally opts for a style in *Maus* which renders the figures minimally, with just dots for eyes and short slashes for eyebrows and mouths. The effect is, as one writer has said, that the characters look "as if they were human beings with animal heads pasted on them."[20] The masklike quality of the drawings becomes part of the text itself when the mouse-Jews disguise themselves by

Figure 10. Art Spiegelman, rejected "woodcut" drawing for *Maus*
© Art Spiegelman

wearing masks which bear the pig-faces that indicate Gentile Poles in *Maus*. Readers can see the strings holding the masks on, yet the characters themselves take no notice. Though the mouse faces are often blank, with few individual attributes, Spiegelman is able to make each Jewish character, at least, distinct and recognizable. (The faces of the Nazi cat-soldiers are usually hooded by their coal-scuttle helmets.) Differences in the characters are indicated not by facial features but by more general pictorial techniques—gestures, posture, and clothing. Spiegelman performs subtle wonders of characterization and expression using only two dots for eyes and two lines for eyebrows, and the unobtrusive quality of his drawing is one of its strengths. The rejected woodcut style contained so much information as to trap the reader's gaze within individual panels. But the more open and spare panels of *Maus* allow one's eye to flow smoothly from scene to scene, and we fail to sense that we are constantly being manipulated into reading at a predetermined pace.[21]

In the panel of the betrayal in the chandelier bunker the differences between the first "Maus" and the book version demonstrate how Spiegelman's later approach tries to eschew overt prejudgments about the characters and the episodes. In "Maus" (figure 11) the turncoat mouse has a hooked nose, his shaded eyes echo the malevolent expressions of the cats, and he points to the hidden mice with a beclawed finger. The faces of the mice are dominated by their large oval eyes with black pupils, and one of them sheds a tear as the Jew whom they helped turns them over to the exterminators.

In the final version, the informer's face is nearly averted so that we cannot see his expression, and his pointing finger is a much more neutral gesture. The mice are no longer squashed beneath the attic roof, as in the first version; they sit upright, dismayed but not terrified at their betrayal. The Gestapo cats, while still threatening in demeanor, are more equal in size to the mice, and their expressions are less stereotypically villainous than in the "Maus" panel. For all its simplicity of line, the *Maus* panel (figure 12) is a more sophisticated sequential art device. The Nazi's harsh command ("Juden Raus!") physically links the two halves of the composition and leads the eye up from the Nazis in the lower room to the mice looking down from the attic; the split caption forces a reader to move back down to the bottom of the panel, emphasizing the sequence of events. Thus even though the *Maus* panel is much less detailed, the experience of reading it is more dynamic and controlled than in the rather static "Maus" version.

Figure 11. Art Spiegelman, "Maus," page 2
© Art Spiegelman

Figure 12. Art Spiegelman, *Maus*, page 113
© Art Spiegelman

Beast Fables and the Not-So-Funny Animals

The central difference between "Maus" and *Maus* is that the first version is an allegory, thinly disguised at best, while the second is an animal comic book. The distinction makes all the difference. That is, though anthropomorphized animal cartoons and comics undoubtedly trace their formal origins to beast fables and folktales, the "funny animal" genre of comics has developed its own distinctive, peculiar conventions and metaphysics.[22] Most readers of *Maus* have struggled to understand how a Holocaust comic book can be so compelling and why the unlikely genre of "talking animals" seems so paradoxically appropriate. Many reviewers have attributed the book's undeniable power to Spiegelman's representational strategy and have cited sources and antecedents for depictions of humans as animals which range from medieval Jewish illuminated manuscripts to Walt Disney's Mickey Mouse.[23] But while *Maus* extends the possibilities of sequential art, it does not repudiate the heritage of its comic-book form, and to understand how the animal metaphor in *Maus* works requires a consideration of the traditions of "funny animal" comics.

Some of the greatest achievements in American popular culture have used animal characters. Walt Disney's world-famous characters Mickey Mouse and Donald Duck dominated animated cartoons for decades, but Otto Mesmer's Felix the Cat, and Bugs Bunny and Daffy Duck, among many others from the Warner Brothers studio, were likewise central to the development of American animation. In newspaper comic strips, George Herriman's *Krazy Kat* and Floyd Gottfredson's *Mickey Mouse* were only the most prominent of scores of animal comics; Walt Kelly's gently satiric *Pogo* began as a comic book before moving to the newspaper comics page.

Perhaps the best animal comic books of all are the works of Carl Barks, creator of that preeminent cartoon capitalist Uncle Scrooge and the writer and artist of hundreds of *Donald Duck* and *Uncle Scrooge* stories for more than twenty years. Barks's Donald Duck is a very different character from the short-fused blowhard of Disney's animated cartoons. His hot temper remains, but the comic-book Donald is a complex person whose humorous misadventures arise out of his intrepidity, his curiosity, and his emotional bonds to his nephews and to his rich uncle. The keyword here is "person." Barks always conceived of Donald as a human being who happened to be shaped like a duck, and this curious indifference to the animal nature of the characters is a distinguishing mark of the "funny animal" tradition in popular narratives.

In traditional animal fables, human characteristics are abstracted and projected onto animals; George Orwell's *Animal Farm* is a sophisticated modern version of this allegorical tradition. Beast fables link into a system of well-established correspondences based on the natural attributes of species; foxes are cunning, wolves voracious, mules stubborn, cats curious, and so on. The specific qualities may vary according to the thematic function of the animal character or to fit cultural conventions about the particular animal, but the quality itself is central to the animal's narrative role. The "funny animal" genre takes these allegorical meanings as a starting point but then proceeds to ignore, qualify, or reverse them. For example, the "mouse-ness" of Mickey Mouse is only tangentially related to his essential character. It suggests that he is nonthreatening (Mickey could not be a wolf, for instance), but he is not timid or sneaky, nor does he live in a hole. Mickey's arch-enemy is Black Pete, a cat, but Pete often allies himself with dogs and even monkeys. In the animated cartoon *Tom and Jerry*, the basic premise is the archetypal antagonism of cats and mice, but the stories themselves usually revolve around the discovery by the cat and the mouse that they need each other.

In *Krazy Kat*, the giddy surrealism of the strip begins with the reversal of traditional animal qualities; the cat loves the mouse, the dog loves the cat, and the mouse aggressively attacks the cat. Where the beast fable uses animal characters to engage an elaborate language of conventional meanings, the "funny animal" genre often uses those meanings only to establish relations among the characters, and the "animalness" of the characters becomes vestigial or drops away entirely. (Thus Donald Duck has no wings and cannot fly without an airplane.) Mickey Mouse poses a conundrum of animal metaphor; his friend, Goofy, is a dog, but he also owns an appropriately canine pet, Pluto. In this case, the species are subordinate to their relation; Mickey is essentially a man, and Pluto is "man's best friend."

Animal comic books have generally been aimed at young readers, and their predominant mode is humor. But *Maus* is not the first animal comic for adults. The underground comix gleefully plundered all the comic-book genres, and the animal comics came in for their share of appropriation and parody. The most notorious example is *Air Pirates Funnies* (1971), in which a number of comix artists depicted Disney animal characters such as Mickey and Minnie Mouse taking drugs and having sex.[24] Many other comix artists exploited the animal comics for their own ends.[25]

The most thorough exploration of the conventions of animal comics comes in the work of Robert Crumb, whose *Fritz the Cat* became one of the only underground comix characters to cross over into the popular media when Ralph Bakshi produced an animated feature based on the character.[26] Other Crumb animal characters include Those Cute Little Bearzy Wearzies, Dirty Dog, and Fuzzy the Bunny. The comix transmutation of the talking animals genre into the "not-so-funny animals"[27] culminates in stories such as Crumb's "The Goose and the Gander Were Talking One Night."[28]

In this story a suburban husband and wife discuss modern anxieties as they put their children to bed, share a cup of tea, take a walk, and watch the late show on television. The details of the setting are quintessentially bourgeois, with mismatched chairs around the kitchen table and homemade potholders hanging above the stove. But the characters themselves are geese; their feathery tails protrude from the backs of their jeans. They are aware that they are animals (the husband says, "I'm a pretty average guy... just your normal everyday goose...."), but they think of themselves as human, too. The angst-ridden father says, "Why do I think we're doomed? Oh, I dunno.... It's everything, I guess.... Just the way the human race keeps going head-on with population and technology an' all that...." The basic metaphor in "The Goose and the Gander Were Talking One Night" functions as does the mouse-metaphor in Spiegelman's work.

In Crumb's story, the father's feeling of helplessness in the face of the "collapse of this man-made system of things" makes him feel as if he were as silly and ineffectual as a goose. His gooseness becomes part of the furniture of the story, enabling us to see past the intentional banality of the setting and conversation to the real-life situation it depicts; we are aware that these are talking geese even as we ignore the fact. Here, as in many of his animal stories, Crumb superimposes the conventions of animal comics onto a mundane and threatening modern world. In *Maus*, Spiegelman's extension of the animal metaphor from Crumb's kind of satiric social commentary into history, biography, and autobiography was made possible by the underground comix, which first showed that the "funny animals" could open up the way to a paradoxical narrative realism.[29]

There is something almost magical, or at least mysterious, about the effect of a narrative that uses animals instead of human characters.[30] The animals seem to open a generic space into a precivilized innocence in which human behavior is stripped down to a few essential qualities, and irrelevancies drop away; as Spiegelman says, using animals becomes "a much more direct way of dealing with the material."[31] In *Maus*, the initial premise of cats and mice effectively presents the power relations between the Nazis and the Jews, and it suggests as well the predatory nature of the Nazi oppression. It makes the term "extermination" resonate powerfully, and deepens too the scenes of Jews in hiding, as in Spiegelman's chapters "Mouse Holes" and "Mouse Trap."

The metaphor also raises some problems. Given that cats chase mice in the course of the natural order, if we thoroughly apply the animal metaphor to *Maus*, the Nazi Final Solution can be seen not as a moral collapse of cosmic proportions but as a logical and necessary acting out of natural roles. But the animal metaphor in *Maus* functions simply as a premise to be absorbed and then put out of mind; we respond to characters who are human beings, not animals. Says Spiegelman, "The metaphor is meant to be shucked like a snakeskin."[32] *Maus* attempts always to allow its readers to make the moral judgments, and the animal metaphor does not extend so far as to grant moral absolution to one side or the other.

The tenuousness of the metaphor appears at the many times it is broken or calls attention to itself. For example, the Spiegelmans fail to remark on the human figures in "Prisoner on the Hell Planet." In one remarkable episode, as Vladek and his wife are hiding in a cellar, Anja screams that rats are crawling on her. Vladek replies, "Those aren't rats. They're very small. One ran over my hand before. They're just *mice!*" The story returns to the present as Vladek tells Art, "Of course, it *was* really rats. But I wanted to make Anja feel more easy."[33] The panel set in the past and the one in the present are linked by the figure of a large, realistically drawn rat with a malevolent expression. The incident stresses that the Jews and Nazis are mice and cats only in relation to each other; the metaphor is a way of seeing humans, not a literal characterization.

In the first section of *Maus, Part II: From Mauschwitz to the Catskills* (figure 13), Spiegelman addresses directly the nature of the metaphor. In a wonderfully self-reflexive and comic passage, Art's wife, Françoise, finds him sketching and asks what he's doing. Art replies, "Trying to figure out how to draw you. . . ."

"Want me to pose?"
"I mean in my book. What kind of *animal* should I make you?"
"Huh? A *mouse*, of course!"
"But you're *French!*"

Figure 13. Art Spiegelman, *Maus*, Part II, page 154
© Art Spiegelman

"Well ... How about a bunny rabbit?"

Nah. Too sweet and gentle."

HMMPH."

"I mean the French in general. Let's not forget the centuries of anti-Semitism....

"I mean, how about the Dreyfus Affair? The Nazi collaborators! The—"

"*Okay!* But if you're a mouse, I ought to be a mouse too. I *converted,* didn't I?"[34]

Throughout this scene Françoise is, of course, already drawn as a mouse. The passage emphasizes that the metaphor is a conscious device applied by the artist; *we* see the characters as mice and cats, but they perceive themselves as humans. Spiegelman uses the animal metaphor to evoke general associations of predation, extermination, and bestiality, not to assign a set of allegorical meanings to his text.

History as Autobiography

Jack Jackson's histories support their claim to truth by means of their realistic, quasi-photographic rendering style, their convincing, if unconventional, dialogue, and the documentary evidence that surrounds the text in the appendixes and suffuses the narrative within the panels. Art Spiegelman takes a different tack; a Holocaust narrative with mice and cats as characters cannot pretend to be a documentary. *Maus* relies on the personal situation of Art and Vladek to make good its truth claim; Vladek's is the authenticity of an eyewitness, while Art has a psychological need to hear and render the truth. Art's role as an interlocutor is crucial to the narrative. Since Art evinces little historical knowledge to start with, Vladek must explain, to Art and to us, the specific details of how the process of the Holocaust worked, and these details are one of the book's great strengths. As one reviewer says:

> Spiegelman makes the bureaucratic sadism of the Germans uncannily vivid—all the steps and reroutings and sortings and resortings that preceded mass murder. *Maus* is a work of hyperrealist detail. Nobody could have anticipated that a comic book about the Holocaust could have told so much about the way this particular endgame was played out: precisely how the black market worked within the ghettos; exactly what happened, in sequence, when the Germans occupied a town; why in 1943 a Jew would have thought Hungary a haven, and how he would have tried to get his family there.[35]

Gopnik is right about the vividness of Spiegelman's treatment of his material, but it should be no surprise that sequential art can explain the sequence of events so clearly. The linked but separate boxes in comics have always lent themselves to process analysis, and "how-things-work" comics are an important subgenre of educational comic books.[36]

What *Maus* does do in an unprecedented way for a comic book is to combine seemingly disparate genres and narrative approaches into a single seamless story. The funny animal overlay on history is a bold move, as we have seen, yet *Maus* does even more; it makes Vladek's Holocaust story and Art's psychological quest into a single narrative which blends public and private history. These two strains emerge early in *Maus*, in one of the book's most problematic passages. Vladek describes to Art how, as a young man in Czestochowa, Poland, he dated a local girl and eventually threw her over for Anja Zylberberg, who became Art's mother. Vladek tells Art that he doesn't want the story of his bachelor amours in Art's book, saying, "It has nothing to do with Hitler, with the Holocaust!" Art protests, "But Pop—it's great material. It makes everything more real—more human. I want to tell *your* story, the way it really happened." Vladek says, "But this isn't proper, so respectful.... I can tell you other stories, but such private things, I don't want you to mention." Art finally acquiesces, "Okay, okay—I promise."[37] But of course, the story is in the book anyway.

Art and Vladek never discuss this subject later, and nothing within the text indicates that Vladek ever relented. This apparent betrayal of Vladek's trust is troubling if we simply identify the cartoonist with the author of *Maus*, and we have grounds for doing so. The biographical blurb on the book's jacket features a self-portrait by Art Spiegelman: the mouse-cartoonist working at his drawing board. But the animal metaphor immediately distances the narrator from the real-life author; Art Spiegelman is not a mouse. The ambiguity appears in interviews when Spiegelman speaks of "the mouse cartoonist" and his "mouse parents."[38] Any writer, even (or especially) an autobiographer, creates a fictional persona when he or she begins to write. In autobiographical comics, where the writer imagines not simply a verbal "I" but a physical figure for his own character, the relation between writer and narrator becomes even more complex. The ineluctable fictionality of any narrative, even the most thoroughly "objective" history or autobiography, allows a shifting identification between author and character; Art Spiegelman is a cartoonist and his father is a Holocaust survivor, but neither is a mouse made of ink, even though *Maus* asks us to believe that they are, and the book succeeds when we acquiesce. "Realism" thus becomes a conspiracy between writer and reader, not an essential relation between certain texts and the world of experience.

Spiegelman points to this inescapable discrepancy between text and world in the latest installment of *Maus.* As Art and Françoise drive toward the Catskills in response to a desperate call from Vladek, Art worries that his work in progress is "presumptuous," saying, "I mean, I can't even make any sense of my relationship with my father.... How am I supposed to make any sense out of *Auschwitz!* ... of the *Holocaust!*"[39] In a soliloquy lasting eleven panels on two pages, Art pours out his fears and insecurities, with only an occasional comment from his wife. In the last four panels Art directly addresses the problem of imagining and representing the Holocaust.

> Sigh. I feel so inadequate trying to reconstruct a reality that was worse than my darkest dreams.
>
> And trying to do it as a *comic strip!*—I guess I bit off more than I can chew. Maybe I ought to forget the whole thing.
>
> There's so much I'll never be able to understand or visualize. I mean reality is too *complex* for comics....
>
> FRANÇOISE: Just keep it honest, honey.
>
> See what I mean.... In real life you'd *never* have let me talk this long without interrupting.
>
> Hmmph. Light me a cigarette.[40]

When Art implicitly betrays his promise to his father, the incident fits perfectly with the characterization of the narrator throughout *Maus.* If Vladek takes no pains to retouch his own actions in the Holocaust story, the writer of *Maus* is careful to show Art's failures as well; the cartoonist is more concerned with writing his book than with protecting his father's feelings. At the very end of the published *Maus,* Art learns that Vladek has destroyed Anja's journal of her wartime experiences which she was saving to give to her son. Art, who has been searching for these diaries to give a balanced perspective to his parents' story, explodes in anger and frustration: "God *DAMN* You! You—you murderer! How the hell could you do such a thing!!" The book ends with Art walking away after a partial reconciliation with his father, muttering, "... Murderer."[41]

Though the tensions between Art and Vladek are unresolved at the book's stopping point, the motivations of both characters are clear and convincing. Vladek burned Anja's papers in a fit of grief after her suicide, and *Maus* has made clear how painful her death was to her husband. For Art, the writing of the Holocaust book has become his closest connection to his parents; his mother's writings represent for him much more than just documentary support for his project. In a book about mass death, Art's outburst, "Murderer!" resonates back through the story. In "Prisoner on the Hell Planet," Art accuses his mother of psychologically murdering him by killing herself; now he blames Vladek for killing Anja, perhaps figuratively by destroying her words, but perhaps more literally by driving her to suicide with his miserliness and emotional tyranny.

Moral judgments in *Maus* become extremely dicey indeed. To call Vladek a murderer after hearing of his ordeal at the hands of the Nazis seems shockingly inappropriate, yet Art's patent need to understand his mother's life at least explains his brutal words, if it does not excuse them. At other points in the story, Art's impatience and intolerance with his aging and ailing father are balanced by Vladek's pettiness and insensitivity. For example, when Vladek tries to dragoon Art into repairing the rain gutters on Vladek's house, Art refuses because his father is too cheap to hire a handyman. The result of Spiegelman's presentation of these mixed motivations and conflicting desires is that *Maus* presents no exemplary characters, and the book generates no moral center from within the text to dictate how we must judge either the past story of the Holocaust or the present-day relationship between the mouse-survivor and his mouse-cartoonist son.

Thus *Maus* differs from most other comic-book tellings of history, with their didactic, persuasive, or sensational impulses. For example, Jack Jackson's Texas histories both educate readers about forgotten heroes from the past and confront the origins of problems which have formed our present; Harvey Kurtzman's E.C. antiwar histories use thrilling war stories to argue against the glamorization of militarism. But *Maus* is not an educational comic in the traditional sense of teaching facts; it exploits the familiarity of one of the central events of Western civilization to tell a very personal story. Nor does Spiegelman's approach in *Maus* resemble standard comic-book formulas, such as horror and adventure. The horrific reality of the Nazi extermination camps is ill suited to the often puerile conventions of adventure comics, and even the horror genre usually falls flat when dealing with the overpowering Holocaust material.[42]

What saves *Maus* from trivializing or sentimentalizing its difficult and emotional subject is its often ruthless examination of the
psychologies of Vladek and of Art and the graphic simplicity of
Spiegelman's style. The underground comix included autobiographical and confessional comic-book stories, and as we shall see in the
next chapter, Harvey Pekar recently has transformed autobiographical comic books in his *American Splendor*. But *Maus* is sui generis
in American comics because of the bold way it focuses Vladek's biography and Art's autobiography through the lens of world history.
Art tells Vladek, "I want to tell *your* story, the way it really happened,"[43] then proceeds to depict Vladek's passage through the hell
of the Holocaust in a comic book with Jews and Nazis as mice and
cats. In so doing he embarks on a project which ultimately proves
that sequential art is a medium whose potential for truth-telling is
limited only by the imagination and the honesty of the men and
women who use it.

1. The eventual winner was Donald Howard for his *Chaucer: His Life, His Work,
His World* (New York: Dutton, 1987).

2. Art Spiegelman, *Maus: A Survivor's Tale* (New York: Pantheon Books, 1986).
The chapters of *Maus* were first published serially in *Raw*.

3. Subsequent chapters of *Maus* will appear biannually in *Raw*.

4. Richard Gehr, review of *Maus: A Survivor's Tale*, by Art Spiegelman, *Artforum*,
February 1987, p. 10.

5. Elie Wiesel, "For Some Measure of Humility," *Sh'ma* 5/100 (31 October 1975),
314. Wiesel's statement appears in Alvin Rosenfeld, "The Problematics of Holocaust
Literature," in *Confronting the Holocaust* (Bloomington: Indiana University Press,
1978), 4.

6. T. W. Adorno, "Cultural Criticism and Society," in *Prisms*, trans. Samuel and
Shierry Weber (Cambridge, Mass.: MIT Press, 1981), 34.

7. Jack Fischel and Sanford Pinsker, preface to *Literature, the Arts, and the Holocaust*, Holocaust Studies Annual, vol. 3 (Greenwood, Fla.: Penkevill Publishing,
1987), x.

8. The distance between the author Art Spiegelman and the narrator of *Maus* will
be discussed more fully below. I will refer to the writer as "Spiegelman," the mouse-
character as "Art."

9. *Maus*, 100.

10. Ibid., 103.

11. Art Spiegelman, interview, "Fresh Air," National Public Radio, December 1986.

12. Spiegelman, interview, "Fresh Air."

13. Art Spiegelman and Françoise Mouly, "Jewish Mice, Bubblegum Cards, Comics
Art, and Raw Possibilities," interview by Joey Cavalieri (New York, 1980–1981),
Comics Journal 65 (August 1981):105–106.

14. Spiegelman, interview, "Fresh Air."

15. Reprinted in *Comix Book* no. 2, ed. Denis Kitchen (New York: Magazine Management, 1974):51–53.

16. The "chandelier bunker" episode appears at *Maus*, 113–117.

17. Ibid., 119.

18. Spiegelman and Mouly, "Jewish Mice," 116.

19. Ibid.

20. Harvey Pekar, "*Maus* and Other Topics," *Comics Journal* 113 (December 1986):56.

21. Spiegelman discusses the flow of the text at Spiegelman and Mouly, "Jewish Mice," 116–117.

22. The term "funny animal" is particularly inappropriate in discussions of *Maus*, but it is the most common name for comics featuring anthropomorphized animals; "talking animals" is another. "Genre" too is a problematic term. A Mickey Mouse strip can partake of the "funny animal" genre, the western adventure genre, and the picaresque genre all at once.

23. See, for instance, Adam Gopnik's list of examples in his review "Comics and Catastrophe," *Atlantic Monthly*, 22 June 1987, pp. 29–34.

24. *Air Pirates* was successfully sued by Walt Disney Productions for copyright infringement in a precedent-setting First Amendment case which established limits on the use of copyrighted characters in parodies.

25. Other animal characters in the comix include Gilbert Shelton's superhero parody, *Wonder Wart-hog*, Bob Armstrong's *Mickey Rat*, Bobby London's lecherous *Dirty Duck*, and the absurd picaresque insect *Coochy Cooty* by Robert Williams; the struggle between man and intransigent pet cat was played out in both Jay Lynch's *Nard n' Pat* and Shelton's *Fat Freddy's Cat*. More recently, Reed Waller and Kate Worley's *Omaha the Cat Dancer* continues the underground heritage of animal comix for adults.

26. Crumb took no part in the making of the movie and disavowed it after its release in 1972.

27. The phrase is Richard Gehr's, *Artforum* review, 10.

28. *Best Buy Comics* (San Francisco: Apex Novelties, 1979).

29. Spiegelman himself toyed with the conventions of animal comics in strips such as "Shaggy Dog Story," reprinted in Spiegelman and Mouly, "Jewish Mice."

30. For example, the works of Carl Barks which feature human beings are flat and undistinguished compared with his complex and compelling duck stories.

31. Spiegelman and Mouly, "Jewish Mice," 106.

32. Art Spiegelman, in Ron Mann, director, *Comic Book Confidential* (1988), motion picture.

33. *Maus*, 147.

34. Art Spiegelman, *Maus: A Survivor's Tale*, "Chapter 7: Mauschwitz. Being the beginning of *Maus*, Part II: From Mauschwitz to the Catskills," insert in *Raw* no. 8 (1986):154. (The pagination in *Maus*, Part II is consecutive with that of *Maus*, Part I.)

35. Gopnik, "Comics and Catastrophe," 30.

36. For example, the seminal comic-book creator Will Eisner spent years working on sequential art maintenance manuals for the United States armed forces. More recently, the CIA supplied anti-Sandinista forces in Nicaragua with assassination manuals in comic-book form.

37. *Maus*, 23.

38. Spiegelman, interview, "Fresh Air."

39. *Maus*, Part II, 157.

40. Ibid., 158.

41. *Maus*, Part II, 159.

42. See, for example, Lee Elias and Bill Dubay's "Rebirth," *Epic Illustrated* 23 (April 1984):75, which uses graphic depictions of the death camps to set up a rather hackneyed reincarnation theme. The outstanding comic-book use of the Holocaust is

Bernie Krigstein's stunning tale of paranoia, guilt, and vengeance, "Master Race," from E.C.'s *Impact* no. 1 (March–April 1955), in which a former death-camp commandant, now hiding in America, confronts one of the victims of his brutality on a New York subway.

43. *Maus*, 23.

5

"You Can Do Anything with Words and Pictures": Harvey Pekar's *American Splendor*

American Splendor refuses to fit into any of the main categories of American comic books. This self-published black-and-white magazine-sized comic book is not a superhero or adventure comic, like nearly everything published by the two main comics publishers, Marvel and DC. It doesn't parody or rework traditional comic-book formulas, like most of the black-and-white comics put out by the growing number of "independent" publishers. And despite its roots in the underground comix, *American Splendor* is neither a holdover from the counterculture nor an avant-garde graphics anthology, like Art Spiegelman's *Raw*. It is, simply, "The Life and Times of Harvey Pekar."[1]

In each *American Splendor*, published and distributed annually since 1976 by Pekar himself, Pekar writes stories about his own daily life, depicts anecdotes and conversations he has heard and overheard, dramatizes vignettes from his civil-service job in Cleveland, and presents his often glum ruminations about his career and his life in general. Pekar works full time as a file clerk in Cleveland's Veterans Hospital, and his comic books generally sell about enough copies to break even. Harvey Pekar does not draw his own comics, and in each issue of *American Splendor* he colloborates with several different artists. Pekar's friend and best-known collaborator, Robert Crumb, explains Pekar's creative procedure:

> Usually he writes his story ideas soon after the event, while the nuances of it are still fresh in his mind. He always has a large backlog of these stories, which he can choose from to compose each new issue of *American Splendor*. He writes the stories in a crudely laid-out comic page format using stick figures, with the dialogue over their heads, and some descriptive directions for the artist to work from. The next phase involves calling up various artists and haranging [sic] them to take on particular stories.[2]

The cover blurbs of some individual issues of *American Splendor* reveal both Pekar's self-mocking irony and the comic book's relentlessly quotidian focus: "More Depressing Stories from Harvey Pekar's Hum-Drum Life"; "Stories about Sickness and Old People"; "Big Divorce Issue"; "Life as a War of Attrition." Pekar's stories reverse the traditional escapism of American comic-books; *American Splendor* explores the horrors and adventures of everyday life: facing a dull job on Monday, losing glasses, being called for jury duty, breaking up with a lover.

Pekar's settings are the street corners and workplaces of lower-class Cleveland, his music the cadences of ethnic and working-class speech. Pekar told an interviewer, "I want to write literature that pushes people into their lives rather than helping them escape from them. Most comic books are vehicles for escapism, which I think is unfortunate. I think that the so-called average person often exhibits a great deal of heroism in getting through an ordinary day, and yet the reading public takes this heroism for granted. They'd rather read about Superman than themselves."[3] *American Splendor*, like no other comic book before it, examines and celebrates the agonies and triumphs of individual life. By the standards of mainstream comic books, Harvey Pekar's stories are, as Robert Crumb says, "so staggeringly mundane as to border on the exotic!"[4] The works of Jack Jackson and Art Spiegelman, though daring and original in execution, are extensions of well-established comic-book genres, but Pekar's *American Splendor* takes sequential art into realistic and autobiographical places where comics have almost never been before.

Harvey Pekar specializes in comic-book stories which present his own life in all its ordinariness and which examine his often prickly personality with all its annoying, frustrating, and disagreeable traits. Pekar tries to balance each issue of *American Splendor*, mixing short humorous pieces with long autobiographical stories and philosophical reflections, and his own moods in the stories range from angry paranoia about his personal frustrations to (relatively) cheery optimism about his life as a writer. The stories in *American Splendor* often attempt to present experience as precisely as possible; Pekar says of his approach to realism in comic books: "I try to be as accurate as I possibly can because I want people to identify with my work. For me, I can't go wrong if I get stuff accurate, even if people stumble, fumble around when they're talking. I'm obsessed with getting details accurate. I might employ a linear narrative style in one story and a non-linear style in another, but I'm always trying to be true to the facts."[5]

The diversity of Pekar's narrative approaches is a paradoxical outgrowth of his single-minded autobiographical focus. Pekar uses both first- and third-person narration; some stories are told entirely in captions, some are nearly silent pantomimes, with little or no dialogue. A "Harvey Pekar" figure is not present in every piece in *American Splendor*, yet even in those stories and vignettes that are about other people, the author is present by implication as an observer or listener; when Pekar does not appear, one critic notes, "we understand that we are listening to what Pekar himself overheard."[6] Many of the stories do feature a protagonist named "Harvey Pekar," but Pekar also adopts a number of fictionalized autobiographical personae, including "Herschel," "Our Man," and "Jack the Bellboy." The Pekar character is recognizable by his distinctive characteristics; he is dark-haired with sideburns (and in the later issues a receding hairline), casual if not downright slovenly in dress, usually stoical in expression, and he works at what the persona often calls a "flunky job." Pekar's stories often end ambiguously, with the only conclusion an offhand moral tacked on by the narrator.

The vast distance between what one Pekar-persona calls his "neorealistic style"[7] and the usual concerns and procedures of American comic books appears in stories like "Awaking to the Terror of the New Day."[8] The title points to Pekar's perennial theme of the not-so-quiet desperation of everyday life. The story opens with the protagonist, called here "our man," on the phone with his ex-wife as he complains about his loneliness. He asks if they can see each other again, "sorta on a experimental basis." She tells him that she is seeing someone new, and his pleading turns to bitterness and anger:

"OUR MAN": I shoulda known better than to call. You know I still care about you but you don't give a shit for me.

EX-WIFE: That's not true. I'm concerned about you. I want you to do well. It's just that…

"OUR MAN": Yeah, sure, I've heard it before. Well, lemme tell you somethin', you lousy bitch, with friends like you, I don't need no enemies….

"OUR MAN": … You lousy…

EX-WIFE: That's why I don't want to see you. You haven't changed at all. Well, I don't have to listen to you anymore (click).

Disappointed at the rebuff and disgusted with himself for both his forlorn hope and what he knows to be his foul temper, "our man" wonders what to do next. He's tired of watching television, and the Cleveland winter makes it too cold for him to hang out on the street corner. With nothing else to do, he lies down for a short nap, only to awaken at six the next morning, having slept all night in his clothes. His drab room is cold and he feels jittery, so he masturbates to calm himself down. He tries to think of a fantasy woman, which reminds him of his troubles with "chicks": "It ain't right for asshole chicks t'have good bodies. . . . Hmm, I'll think about Susan. She's good lookin' an' she was real nice t'me, too." His face relaxes as he reaches orgasm, but he feels "sad an' hollow" when he is finished. He needs to get ready for work at his "shit gig," so he gets up, sheds his slept-in clothes, and takes a bath (figure 14). The warm bath is comforting, but he is reluctant to get back out into his cold apartment. As he considers his history of poor jobs, he thinks that a nervous breakdown might be a welcome relief from his routine existence, then realizes that, "If I freaked out I'd have t' start from further back than this."

He finally steels himself and gets out of the tub, only to find that his socks are full of holes and his clothes are falling apart. He eats a breakfast of sugared children's cereal, puts on his coat, walks out into the wintry wind, and slogs his way through the snow to the subway station. All through his morning routine, "our man" keeps up a running internal monologue as he ponders how to find a new girlfriend and get a better job. ("Awaking to the Terror of the New Day" is set before the Pekar-protagonist starts working at his government job as a hospital file clerk.) The final panel shows "our man" planning his new life strategy: "I'll check out the gover'mint gig scene an' think over where I stand with th' chicks I know. Maybe I'm overlookin' someone. T'day's Thursday, tomorra's Friday. Saturday I c'n sleep late."

Figure 14. Harvey Pekar, Greg Budgett, and Gary Dumm, "Awaking to the Terror of the New Day," page 5
© Harvey Pekar

The narrator ends the story with a caption: "Man looks wherever he can for hope." This weakly optimistic closing moral would be simply trite were it not totally undercut by the following story in *American Splendor* no. 3, "Awaking to the Terror of the Same Old Day," where the same protagonist, called "our hero" this time, suffers through a dull and frustrating weekend which reminds him that Saturdays are no panacea for his loneliness and depression.

While *American Splendor* is too varied for any single story to serve as a paradigm, "Awaking to the Terror of the New Day" does display many of Pekar's typical themes and narrative strategies. Pekar's work first drew attention because of his collaboration with the famous comix artist Robert Crumb, but more often in *American Splendor* his stories are drawn by the Cleveland team of Greg Budgett and Gary Dumm. A critic has described their work:

> When Budgett and Dumm work together, which is most of the time, Budgett does the pencil drawings and Dumm inks them. The result is a good, "solid" and essentially traditional comic book style. Pekar refers to their work as having a "strong, funky feel". . . .
>
> Working as a team, Budget and Dumm have appeared in every issue of *American Splendor* except # 4,[9] but in that issue Dumm, working alone, had a seven pager and the back cover. Clearly these two are Harvey's chief collaborators and they, even more than Crumb, give *American Splendor* its special character.[10]

The relatively crude postures and broad brushstrokes of Budgett and Dumm's artwork are peculiarly appropriate to Pekar's brand of low-brow realism. The drawing style in "Awaking to the Terror of the New Day" defines itself by what is not. It avoids the glamorizing foreshortening and hyperbolic muscularity of the superhero comics; here the figures are accurately proportioned, and the perspectives generally are from eye level. Budgett and Dumm's drawings lack too the comic exaggerations of the conventional "bigfoot" humor style. (Robert Crumb's is a good example of a "cartoony" style, although his recent experiments with a brushstroke technique in *American Splendor* are more realistic.)

In "Awaking to the Terror of the New Day," the awkward posture of "our man" as he gets into bed conveys his emotional unease, just as his corpselike positioning after his masturbation reinforces the hollowness he feels. While a more sophisticated use of shading and cross-hatching might make the textures in the story more conventionally "realistic," the blunt lines and simple surfaces of Budgett and Dumm's rendering create a drab and dilapidated visual counterpart to "our man's" depression and alienation.

Though the themes and motifs of "Awaking to the Terror of the New Day" are characteristic of *American Splendor,* Pekar's emphases have shifted somewhat since 1978; rarely in recent years does "our man" find himself in such desperate economic and emotional straits. In addition, the protagonist stops calling women "chicks," and as Pekar further develops his own approach to comic books as opposed to the underground comix, he tends to avoid writing explicitly sexual incidents like the masturbation scene. But remaining constant in Pekar's work are "our man's" hot temper, his problematic relations with women, his reclusiveness, his transcendental cheapness (he's upset at the poor condition of his clothes, not because he wants to look good or keep warm, but because, "I hate t' spend money on clothes"), and his habit of eating junk food. Pekar is more than willing to make himself look unpleasant in the interest of verisimilitude; as he says, "People are always talking about me being cheap, gloomy, inconsiderate, and having a bad temper. It would be crazy for me to whitewash myself. In that case nobody would want to look at my stuff; they couldn't relate to it."[11]

Pekar also continues to use the strategy of presenting a seemingly arbitrary stretch of time in his stories; "Awaking to the Terror of the New Day" ends at the subway station, not because the action has risen to a state of tension which has then been resolved, but because "our man's" immediate train of thought has ended. Like many of Pekar's stories, this one emphasizes the physical details of everyday life; no matter how abstruse the philosophical speculation becomes in *American Splendor,* the world of decaying plaster and kiddie cereals is not far away. For example, "our man's" bath takes up twelve panels; the scene is stretched out over three pages in which the protagonist sits in his bathtub, gets out, shivers, and looks into his sock drawer. With its subtly shifting panel breakdowns and the precise verbal flow of "our man's" complaints and ruminations, the scene reads smoothly and plausibly.

The artwork makes subtle and effective verbal/visual connections: "our man" thinks about his "crib that's falling apart" as his blank gaze leads to a hole in the plaster wall; the perspective wittily shifts to include the toilet behind his head as he thinks, ". . . an' no relief in sight." But to comic-book readers who are accustomed only to brightly colored breakneck fight scenes between cosmos-spanning power figures with the fate of the universe at stake, "our man's" morose toilette in lower-class Cleveland, Ohio, must seem very small beer indeed. Perhaps Harvey Pekar's most startling innovation in the comic-book form is not that he bases his stories on real life but that, in the search for an accurate and believable rendering of experience, he is willing to write stories that can be as drab, depressing, and tedious as life itself. Pekar's aesthetic of aggressively humdrum realism struggles against the tide of decades of comic-book fantasy and escapism.

Still, autobiographical and confessional stories have been written in comic books before *American Splendor*, almost solely in the underground comix.[12] The stylistic expansion of the underground comix artists, especially of the former Clevelander Robert Crumb, helped to inspire Pekar to work in the comic-book form. Pekar says, "All these guys who were doing this stuff, the underground cartoonists, were involved in the hippie subculture. And I thought, why can't you do stuff about everyday life, the life that I'm leading. And I said, 'Absolutely nothing.' Comics should not be considered a limited medium."[13] Pekar's emphasis on realistically drawn figures and open-ended slice-of-life vignettes makes *American Splendor*'s tone quite different from the hyperbolic self-dramatization of most personal stories in the undergrounds.

For instance, perhaps the best example of autobiography in the comix is *Binky Brown Meets the Holy Virgin Mary*, Justin Green's confessional memoir of the neuroses caused by a traumatizing Roman Catholic education.[14] Green opens the book with "A Confession to My Readers," showing the artist chained naked and upside down, drawing the comic with a pen held in his teeth and an ink bottle labeled "Dad's blood" by his side while a record player plays a warped version of "Ave Maria" in the background. *Binky Brown* hilariously tells how Green's autobiographical persona, the adolescent Binky Brown, struggles to reconcile his awakening sexuality with the strictures of the Catholic Church.

Unable to repress his taboo "impure thoughts," Binky falls prey to bizarre obsessions and paranoid hallucinations in which his bodily members give off phallic rays that threaten to defile churches for miles around him. Guilt and sin have rarely been evoked in any medium with such wild self-laceration and absurd humor, and *Binky Brown* is one of the classics of the comic-book form. But though Green shares with Harvey Pekar an impulse toward psychological self-examination and brutally honest soul baring, Green's comically extravagant surrealism has more in common with the rest of the unfettered undergrounds than with Pekar's sometimes dour, often ironic rendering of immediate experience.

Precisely how Pekar's approach to *American Splendor* differs from the underground comix can be explained by considering the autobiographical stories of the ubiquitous Robert Crumb. Crumb and Pekar first met in Cleveland in 1962, before Crumb's comic-book work had been published, and Crumb was instrumental in getting Pekar's first comic-book stories published in the undergrounds in 1972.[15] Many of Crumb's stories at least profess to be about his own life, and the bespectacled and mustached artist is a familiar figure to readers of Robert Crumb's own underground comics. Crumb often directly addresses the reader, as in his parodic defense of his controversial depictions of women, "And Now, A Word to You Feminist Women";[16] the artist-figure is the protagonist of a number of other stories, such as "The Adventures of R. Crumb Himself,"[17] "My Troubles with Women,"[18] "The Confessions of R. Crumb," and "The R. Crumb ucke$$ Story."[19]

Pekar too sometimes writes stories in which an autobiographical persona addresses the reader, but when Crumb cannot resist transforming his personal stories into self-parodies and shameless fantasies, Pekar's commitment to straightforward candor and direct rendering of experience keeps his stories serious in tone and realistic in style. An example of what Pekar does *not* do is his collaborator's ironic "The Confessions of R. Crumb." The story opens with the artist at his drawing board, cheerily looking out at us as he explains his artistic and commercial success. His wastebasket is stuffed with lucrative offers from publishers and agents; an arrow points to it with the label, "Notice: R. Crumb does not sell out!"

As Crumb praises freedom of expression in America, an American flag appears behind him, and he lapses into jingoistic patriotic slogans as a pair of Mickey Mouse ears sprout from his head and he sings a verse from "This Land is Your Land." Soon, a vaudeville emcee who looks like Groucho Marx kicks him through a set of doors marked "Hi! Welcome to Crumbland," and the artist realizes that "the wonderful world of R. Crumb turns out to be nothing but an endless black void!!" The blackness becomes his mother's womb, and he emerges a bloody infant complete with glasses and a mustache. The story ends as a juvenile Crumb, wearing a schoolboy uniform and carrying a Roy Rogers briefcase, vows to get his revenge: "Someday when I'm a big man, they'll be sorry!!"[20]

In Harvey Pekar's "American Splendor Assaults the Media," drawn by Robert Crumb, Pekar too addresses the reader to rant about his lack of commercial success and to wallow (like Crumb, always with a sharp sense of self-irony) in self-pity.[21] But Crumb, naturally enough for such a gifted draftsman, habitually conceives of his life and problems in terms of images (the "Crumbland" theme park; the return to the womb; big-legged, large-buttocked women as sex objects); Pekar explains *his* difficulties (figure 15) in front of a plain dark background as he is surrounded by masses of words that confine and oppress him. The visual dimension of the story is still crucial; the images and the jagged page layout support and ratify Harvey's poverty and anger, and the panels focus attention on the figure of Harvey himself. A maniacal-looking Harvey is disgusted to find that the *Village Voice* has hired what he believes to be an inferior cartoonist, even though the editors claimed to be interested in his work; Harvey sits in a warehouse amid boxes of unsold issues of *American Splendor*, pounding his fist in frustration; Harvey glares out at the reader with beetled brow, wearing a ripped T-shirt.

Harvey's diatribe against the calumny of editors and the cheapness of promises ends, not with a sex fantasy, as does Crumb's story, but with an explanation of why he writes *American Splendor:*

> I was gonna write this jive woman a nasty letter, but a guy at work talked me out of it...
>
> FRIEND: Wadda you wanna do that for? They'll just laugh at you.... They'll think you're a crank.... They don't care about you....
>
> So I sublimated by writing this.... That's about what I can do when things bother me—write stories about them....

Where comix artists such as Justin Green and Robert Crumb turn their personal difficulties and psychological struggles into surrealistic high farce, Harvey Pekar at first considers venting his rage. Then he turns his anger into language.

Like his friend Crumb, Harvey Pekar is bothered by many things, and he *is* something of a crank. His stories show him to be frugal to the point of miserliness (and in the past, to the point of petty larceny), easily irritated at everything from old Jewish ladies in supermarkets to the American legal system, sloppily dressed, manic, inconsiderate, and crabby. He is also an extraordinarily keen observer with an eye for the everyday surrealism of human behavior. Pekar collects jazz records and writes articles and reviews for some of the leading American jazz magazines, and he brings a musician's ear to

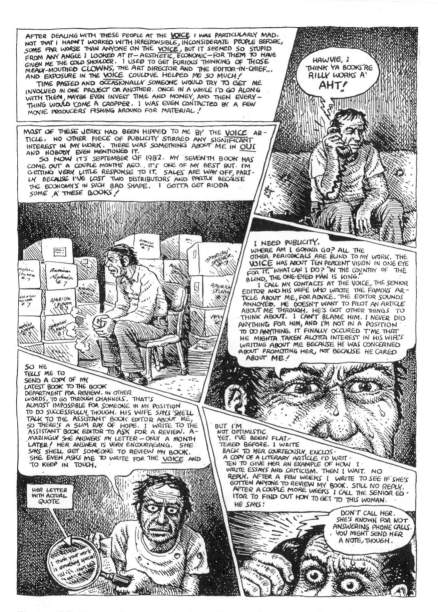

Figure 15. Harvey Pekar and Robert Crumb, "American Splendor Assaults the Media," page 3
© Harvey Pekar

the rhythms of daily speech and the nuances of ethnic dialects; many of the short pieces in *American Splendor* are simply celebrations of the way people talk.

Where Jack Jackson inserts contemporary diction into historical stories to counteract their distancing "pastness," Pekar uses the precision of his ear to convince us that his stories happened exactly as he tells them. Pekar is also a voracious reader. Though his formal schooling lasted only a year beyond high school, Pekar has educated himself about literature, history, and economics by an intensive regime of self-imposed study. He has written for various publications on popular culture, African history, and socialism, and has published discussions of writers such as George Ade, Herman Melville, Mark Twain, Stephen Crane, and Frank Norris.

Pekar's critical concentration on the masters of American realism indicates the wellsprings of his home-grown aesthetic. Though Pekar is familiar with the history and traditions of comics, his approach in *American Splendor* is closer to the realists of prose literature than to anything that has appeared in comic books before. Pekar sometimes pays direct homage to his literary influences. In "Grubstreet, U.S.A.," Pekar draws a parallel between his own efforts to find an audience for *American Splendor* and the struggles of the novelist George Gissing in Victorian England: "God, these guys can't make any money unless they write commercial crap. They live hand-to-mouth, they're looked down on by middle class an' upper class people. . . ."[22] Pekar realizes he could be describing himself but then undercuts his own self-dramatization when he thinks of the security he has from his civil-service day job: "I don't wanna exaggerate, though. I had the advantage over those funky Victorian writers in one big way, so y'don't have to feel as sorry for me as I do for myself. (However, I'd appreciate as much pity as you can give me.)"[23] The one-page story "Katherine Mansfield" is Pekar's internal monologue about Mansfield, mortality, and his own place in literature. The story, drawn by Gary Dumm, shows Harvey sitting in a chair reading Mansfield's *Bliss*. He thinks:

> Some of her stories are almost flawless. She had so much going for her— sensitivity, a fine appreciation of irony, excellent technique, a strong intellect, broad vein of lyricism.... dead at thirty-four.

> What kinda woman was she? Would it've been a letdown t'meet her? She'd have t'be something else in person to measure up to her writing.

All these writers that say so much to me: her, George Eliot, Balzac, all dead. I got an advantage—I'm alive. It's my time now; I'm the one doing the living.... But not forever. I got about thirty years if I get my quota. Everything over that is gravy. I know it; I'm not cocky just because I'm still breathing.

Here were these people, thinking so profoundly, feeling passionately, seeing so much. Their books are my great companions, but reading them is like looking through a one way window.

The story ends with Harvey looking through a doorway, his back to the reader, thinking, "Will anyone at all read my stuff after I'm dead? Will they wonder what kind of guy I was?"[24] The strip has almost no action; Harvey sits and reads, gets up, and thinks. The structure of Harvey's thoughts indicates Pekar's typical concerns. He moves from a literary analysis of Mansfield's writing to the facts of her life, and thence to his own life and work.

His self-absorption might seem at first to be simply banal or narcissistic, and some of his stories do flirt with sentimental self-indulgence. But Pekar's commitment to the standards of realism finally justify, to him and to most of his readers, his self-centered focus. When asked why he writes autobiographically, Pekar says, "Well, I may have a bigger ego than most people—that's for others to decide—but the main reason I write autobiographically is because I find it hard to understand why I myself do things, let alone why others do them. I want my writing to be as accurate and plausible as possible."[25]

For Pekar, accuracy and plausibility in his comic books is entirely consistent with the tenets of literary realism. He deals with immediate experience, physical details, specific actions, and the ethical consequences of everyday life. In his stories he emphasizes character, both his own and that of the people he meets, and, like realists such as Stephen Crane and Sinclair Lewis, he writes stories populated almost entirely by the lower and middle classes. His writing style usually eschews the neat packaging of traditional plot; his stories often seem to be all middle and no ending. This is hardly startling stuff for prose fiction, but in the traditionally escapist and formulaic medium of sequential art, to imitate Balzac and George Eliot is an avant-garde move.

Though many of Pekar's short pieces look very much like gag comic strips, they usually end on a reflective or ambiguous note.

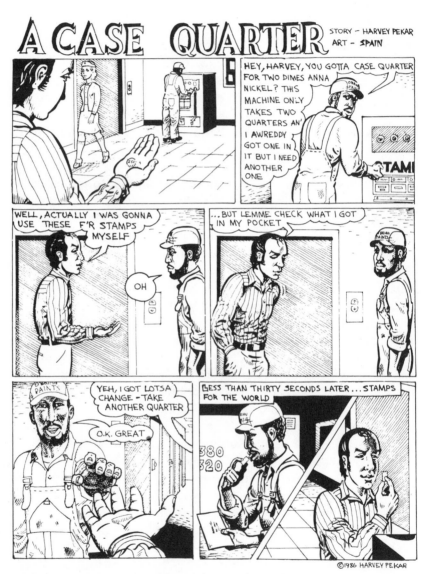

Figure 16. Harvey Pekar and Spain Rodriguez, "A Case Quarter"
© Harvey Pekar

Readers accustomed to the iron-bound Aristotelean structure of the standard three-panel newspaper strip often simply miss the point of Pekar's stories. Says Pekar, "I try to avoid pat endings; plot means nothing to me."[26] Pekar's approach to incident is essentially atmospheric, meant to evoke the chance encounters and dimly apprehended meanings of daily life. For example, the one-page "A Case Quarter" (figure 16)[27] shows Harvey holding change in his palm as he approaches a postage stamp vending machine at the hospital where he works. A workman already at the machine asks, "Hey, Harvey, you gotta case quarter for two dimes anna nickel? This machine only takes two quarters an' I awreddy got one in but I need another one." Harvey tells him, "Well, actually I was gonna use these f'r stamps myself." Harvey checks his pockets, finds more change, and gives the man a quarter. The final panel is split diagonally into two parts, with each man heading in an opposite direction, both looking satisfied as they hold their stamps. The narrative caption reads, "Less than thirty seconds later . . . stamps for the world."

This story is indeed an imitation of a completed action, and the three tiers constitute a beginning, middle, and end, but Aristotle might well question the magnitude of the incident, and "A Case Quarter" has no climactic punch line that would be recognized on the newspaper comics page. The emphasis here is on the speech of the characters, especially the distinctive phrase "case quarter," as the title indicates. The slang adjective "case" denotes a thing which completes a series (as in "case ace," the last ace in a deck of cards being dealt). As the parodic universalizing of the narrative voice suggests, the theme of this vignette is the way people help to complete each other's lives in small and almost unnoticed ways.

Pekar has published dozens of such one-page stories, and in them he is usually more concerned with accurately rendering daily speech than with making formal jokes. When the stories in *American Splendor* do have punch lines, it is usually when the people around Pekar fall habitually or unconsciously into comic modes of presenting themselves, as in "The Last Supper" (figure 17), drawn by Robert Crumb.[28] The master comedian Crumb often draws the traditionally humorous stories by Pekar as opposed to the more autobiographical or reflective parts of *American Splendor.* In "The Last Supper," a slouching office worker named Rudy is late to work. Rudy explains that his father died in the middle of last night's supper and that his mother is mad at him. A woman asks why, and Rudy replies dead-

Figure 17. Harvey Pekar and Robert Crumb, "The Last Supper"
© Harvey Pekar

pan, "UH... I asked if I could finish his pudding...." Though the ironic title and the blackly humorous punch line make this a gag strip, the story combines vaudeville slapstick with a visual character study of an office oddball. The story emphasizes the workaday atmosphere that Crumb's cartoony drawing style so lovingly evokes: the lounging office worker, the cluttered file cabinets with comic strips taped on the side, the varied expressions of Rudy's listeners.

While many of Pekar's stories and vignettes are funny and interesting in their own right, the repetition of characters and scenes and the accretion of a variety of incidents make reading *American Splendor* a cumulative experience, unlike the self-contained gag strips in the newspapers. In a comic book that is thoroughly rooted in the life of a single person, the relativity of individual identity becomes a major thematic subtext.

In traditional prose autobiography, the author creates an "I" over which he or she at least ostensibly has total control, and this identity usually remains stable in the text. But since Pekar does not draw his own stories, the visual component of his character is continually being interpreted by his artist-collaborators, and these versions of Harvey overlay the fictional personae he adopts for himself. Pekar says: "I think that ultimately it's been an advantage to work with a whole variety of artists. I'm like a casting director. While I may not have the control I'd have if I was drawing the stuff myself, I've got guys that together can cover pretty much the whole gamut, where an individual couldn't. I can get guys that collectively can do things that no one person could do, with all the styles I have to draw from."[29] Despite the singleness of his autobiographical vision and the willed smallness of his arena of action, Harvey Pekar is many people, and in *American Splendor* the sequential art medium embodies in its material form the collaboration of other people in the construction of individual identity.

The variety of "Harvey Pekars" appears overtly in "A Marriage Album" (figure 18).[30] Pekar cites this narratively complex reminiscence as an attempt to translate the prose stream-of-consciousness technique into comic-book form.[31] In "A Marriage Album," the author-figure is called both "Herschel" (Harvey Pekar's Yiddish name) and "Harvey"; his wife is simply called "Joyce." Herschel/Harvey sees his wife off to an appointment, works at writing for a while, then lapses into a reverie about his new marriage. Joyce, meanwhile, tells her part of the story to her friends, and the two halves of the narrative combine in counterpoint to one another.

Figure 18. Harvey Pekar, Joyce Brabner, and Val Mayerik,
"A Marriage Album," page 9
© Harvey Pekar

Harvey and Joyce recall how they met through corresponding about *American Splendor* and, despite personal obstacles (such as Harvey's two previous marriages and his thorny idiosyncrasies), eventually got married. As Joyce flies to Cleveland to meet Harvey in person for the first time, she reflects on what she knows of his appearance. Her thought balloon is filled with eight different versions of Harvey's face, each drawn in the style of the one of the artists who works on *American Splendor:* an angry, sweating Harvey as seen by Robert Crumb, a profile of Harvey in Sue Cavey's elegantly stippled style, a reflective Harvey in Gerry Shamray's impressionist mode. When Joyce meets Harvey, his multiple identities resolve for her into a single real person, but for readers of the story this Harvey is simply another representation in Val Mayerik's fluid line. The stylistic diversity of Pekar's many artist-collaborators, the various fictionalizing personae Pekar adopts, and the wide range of his narrative approaches (slice-of-life vignette, reminiscence, ethnic anecdote, character study of friends and acquaintances, confessional story, philosophical rumination, and others) all serve to keep his comics from being monotonous in tone, despite their steadfast focus on the author himself.

As Pekar has refined what he does best, his own presence in the stories becomes more overt and self-consciously central. For example, Pekar has published one story twice, and the differences between the two versions indicate how his approach has subtly altered. The first version, "Overheard in the Cleveland Public Library: March 21, 1977" (figure 19)[32] is a typical example of Pekar's strips that focus on odd characters and emphasize the offhand weirdness of everyday speech. A raggedly dressed middle-aged man asks a kindly old librarian to evaluate his poetry, so she recommends that he take it to the Cleveland Area Arts Council. The man complains that no one likes his poetry and that he doesn't understand the poems in intellectual magazines such as *Harper's* and the *Atlantic.* Taken aback, the librarian replies, "Sir, there's nothing wrong with writing poetry that rhymes." As the title and the documentary subtitle suggest, this strip strives for a transparently immediate rendering of real speech. The silent author/observer appears only in the right foreground of the first and last panel, and he stands just a little closer to the action than does the reading audience. Gary Dumm's simple, almost crude artwork suggests that no artifice stands between the event and its depiction in Pekar's story.

The second version, "Library Story: Take Two" (figure 20),[33] re-

Figure 19. Harvey Pekar and Gary Dumm, "Overheard
in the Cleveland Public Library"
© Harvey Pekar

Figure 20. Harvey Pekar and Michael T. Gilbert, "Library Story, Take Two"
© Harvey Pekar

verses the focus of the first strip from the would-be poet and the librarian to the figure of the writer himself. Michael T. Gilbert's visual technique is much more sophisticated than Dumm's, both in line and shading and in page and panel layouts. Where the first strip pretended to be a chunk of reality taken directly from the world and rendered without artifice, "Take Two" is placed firmly in the ongoing context of Pekar's life and art. The caption tells us that the scene is linked to the previous story, "The Kissinger Letter:" "Here's our man trying to look up what year he saw Henry Kissinger on a T.V. show called 'Town Meeting of the World.' He stops for a minute to dig a conversation between an old librarian and a shabbily dressed guy who's bugging her about something he wrote." The Pekar-figure, "our man," takes up the foreground of the panel, and the librarian and the man are well in the background. The librarian's words extend all the way across the top of the panel, and the configuration of the balloon physically depicts the words going into the eavesdropper's ears.

The first version is a series of speeches and reactions between the two central characters, and the page layout makes the librarian's double take the physical center of the page. In "Take Two" the exchange between the two is confined to the first two tiers of the page, and the woman's silent reaction shot has been drastically reduced in size and in compositional importance. In its place is a similar shot of "our man" pondering the incident he has just witnessed. Pekar often uses these silent panels to time the rhythms of his stories; he says, "I like to use silent panels for punctuation almost as if I'm an oral storyteller."[34]

In the second telling of the library story, the repetition of the phrase, "There's nothing wrong with writing poetry that rhymes," ensures that the idiosyncrasy of speech is still stressed. But the focus shifts away from the speakers to the writer, who moralizes on the event, "That was nice. When the old lady saw he was serious about his writing, she gave him some encouragement," then wonders about its suitability for one of his stories, "But it sounds like the punchline from a corny old joke." The move of the writer to center stage in this story is not one of simple self-aggrandizement; instead, it indicates how Pekar becomes increasingly comfortable with his role as mediator between experience and its representation.

The centrality of Pekar's guiding consciousness becomes the humorous subject of "A Harvey Pekar Story."[35] In this story, Harvey's friend Jon Goldman stops him on the street and tells him, "I had a

Harvey Pekar story happen to me." Over coffee, Jon tells Harvey about his odd encounter with an old man at an office furniture clearance sale, and the story switches to Jon's point of view. Jon goes into the sale and finds the place deserted; the man running the sale comes out, and they discuss the sale of a filing cabinet. The old man forcefully urges Jon to take some women's underwear for free and tells him that he is liquidating his wife's garment business and that he himself is a surgeon. Jon asks his name, and when the old man replies, "Lapidus," Jon asks him if he is the Morris Lapidus of whom Jon has heard. The old man glares in return, then begins to rant about Morris Lapidus.

> Oh no, not me, not that one. I'm Irving Lapidus, not that one. He's a crook, a goniff. People used to confuse me with him.
>
> He's a thief and they blamed me. You know, one time...

As he continues to rave, Jon excuses himself from the doctor's diatribe, saying he has to get to work. Lapidus tells him, "I'm sorry I took up so much of your time. It's when I think of that Morris. ...Boy he burns me up."

The narrative cuts back to Jon and Harvey sitting in the coffee shop, as Jon asks eagerly, "So wasn't that a Harvey Pekar story?" The story ends with Harvey's reply, "Damn near, Jon, damn near." Jon Goldman is right. This mildly bizarre unearthing of the hidden misery in another person's life is *American Splendor*'s meat and potatoes. The story begins with Jon's chance decision to go into the sale and ends inconclusively, evanescing rather than reaching a climax, like so many of Harvey's stories. But Harvey is right, too. What makes this anecdote "a Harvey Pekar story" is not its oddness but the fact that Jon feels compelled to tell it to Harvey Pekar—and he to us.

As Pekar continues to publish *American Splendor,* the production of the comic book takes up more and more of his life. The publication by Doubleday of the two volumes of collected stories from *American Splendor* brought Pekar national publicity, including several appearances on David Letterman's late-night television talk show. As a result, the stories in *American Splendor* become increasingly self-reflexive at the same time they remain autobiographical. Harvey visits a San Diego comics store for an autograph session in "Jack Dickens' Comic Kingdom";[36] Harvey picks up a new edition of *American Splendor* in "At the Bindery,"[37] and an old doctor at

Harvey's job tries to think of jokes that Harvey can put into his book.[38] "American Splendor Assaults the Media" overtly discusses Pekar's struggles as a writer, of course, and other stories pick up the theme.

In "Hysteria,"[39] Harvey calls the editor of a local Cleveland magazine and harasses her about a review of his book that she has promised. Harvey works himself into a frenzy of paranoia and indignation, then realizes that his shouting into the telephone threatens to overstrain his voice. "Hysteria" ends with a sheepish Pekar waking up and testing his voice, "How d'you sound t'day Harvey, how do you sound t'day?" (the letters are drawn incompletely to signify the weakness of his voice). Longtime readers of *American Splendor* remember that Pekar once lost his voice for several months in 1977, and his inability to communicate severely strained his then recent second marriage.[40] Harvey's anxiety about his voice forces him to rein in his volatile temper, and only if we have read "An Everyday Horror Story" do we fully understand the emotional issues of "Hysteria."

Interlocking stories are only one way *American Splendor* becomes self-referential. An unusual opportunity to gauge a Harvey Pekar story against the event it represents occurs in "Late Night with David Letterman" (figure 21).[41] Pekar first appeared on Letterman's talk show on October 15, 1986, and was invited back for repeat appearances in 1987 and 1988.[42] In his first appearance on television Pekar came across as nervous, defensive, and contentious; he squirmed in his seat, told the studio audience to "shut up," and attacked Letterman for the paucity of the backstage food. Letterman and his audience seemed to enjoy Pekar's manic abrasiveness, but the more serious discussion of Harvey's comic-book writing was unclear and fragmented.

In *American Splendor*, Pekar's story about the television show frames a depiction of the show itself with an explanation of Harvey's attitude toward the appearance. The story opens as Joyce tells Harvey that he has been booked onto the Letterman show. While putting away groceries, Harvey ponders how he will handle himself on television; he absentmindedly puts the detergent into the refrigerator. A few days later, as Harvey walks around thinking of the upcoming show, he considers his strategy for dealing with the condescendingly ironic Letterman:

> No sense in tryin' to talk about anything substantive—all the guy wants t'do is banter an' get laughs... light weight shit.

Figure 21. Harvey Pekar and Gerry Shamray, "Late Night with David Letterman," page 9
© Harvey Pekar

People talk about what a great put down artist he is. Shit… He's just in there with dummies, 'at's why he looks good. I musta rapped with dozens a'faster guys in delicatessens.

Gotta get in his face, take his game away from 'im. Smother 'im from the start.

He's middle class, polite, he don't talk fast. I'll overwhelm 'im—even if'e gets off a good one I'll hit 'im quick with two or three shots—won't give the audience a chance to react to 'im.

Street fighting tactics oughta keep 'im off guard, he ain't useta guys like me. …gotta keep cool enough not to freeze an' forget what I'm sayin' or screw up my timin'.

Looks good on paper. I gotta lotta experience, but not on TV. It worked onna street corner, but will it work on TV?

In New York, just before the show, Harvey scrounges around producer Bob Morton's office for free books and food; he tells Morton that since he's only being paid one hundred dollars, "I need t'get as much free stuff as possible t'make this trip a success." Morton tells him, "Look, Harv, act like you're acting now on the show. Be aggressive." Harvey replies, "Don't worry about a thing man; aggressive is my middle name." Harvey thinks, "Good, he digs my shticks." The frame story here makes clear what no television viewer can know; Harvey's seemingly spontaneous behavior on the Letterman show is a "shtick," planned in advance and approved by the producers.[43]

A comparison of the show and the comic-book story shows that sequential art can approximate some of the effects of television quite well. The rectangular borders of the panels work to frame the action as does the television screen, and both media rely on "camera shots" for their individual perspectives. Gerry Shamray's art sometimes follows the producer's camera angles, and Shamray uses a mixture of panels and borderless pictures to capture the seamlessness of video cuts. He likewise often uses lines leading to dialogue drawn directly on the image, rather than standard dialogue balloons; much of the dialogue in the story comes from the show nearly verbatim. But in overall tone the story is quite different from the show itself. Pekar writes the story as a personal victory, "this sour faced, sloppily dressed file clerk turning the tables on Mr. Condescending Wise Guy."[44] But for those watching the show, Pekar's hyperactive baiting of Letterman *seems* to be less a clever strategy and more the nervousness of an abrasive person on television for the first time.

The rhythm of Pekar's narrative does capture the flow of the show itself, with one major exception. After Pekar and Letterman have a long and argumentative discussion about why Harvey can't make a living as a writer, they move on to *American Splendor* itself. In the comic story, Harvey explains how writing comics is like writing for dramatic media: ". . . Writing comics is similar to writing for the theatre or movies because what it involves is writing dialogue and directions to the actors and directors on the one hand or the illustrators on the other." Letterman responds, "Sure sure," and the two get into brief squabble. Harvey mimics Letterman:

PEKAR: Sure.
LETTERMAN: Relax, relax.
PEKAR: Don' worry about it.
LETTERMAN: You don't worry about it!
PEKAR: I don' worry about it. I got a job.

The story shows Harvey articulating his ideas about comics clearly, only to be cut off by Letterman's brusque, "Sure." Perhaps Pekar's smooth discourse on comic writing and drama is what he meant to say.[45] But a viewer of the actual show sees that, perhaps because the transition from the earlier banter to the serious question is so abrupt, at this point Harvey begins to freeze and lose track of what he is saying, just as he had feared. He stutters, his speech is filled with "uhs," and "mans," and very nearly every other word becomes "y'know." Letterman's interjection of "sure" and "relax" seem meant to help Harvey over his rough spot, and Harvey apparently seizes on Letterman's words to bail himself out of his nervousness.[46] Though this incident in the comic book fails to communicate the nuances of what happened on the show, Pekar does not try to make himself look good in his story. In fact, the panel which shows Harvey telling the booing audience, "Hey, shut up," pictures him looking much more maniacal and angry than on the show, where he is clearly joking.

Of course, in a comparison of the story and the show, the television show cannot serve as a base "reality" by which to judge the verisimilitude of Pekar's story. Both sequential art and video are representational media, and neither medium shows the whole story; the television show misses by necessity Harvey's thoughts and his encounter with the producer, and the comic cannot communicate Pekar's bristling energy, or the way the two men interrupt each other's words, or Harvey's light but raspy voice. Pekar's articles in the *Village Voice* and the *Cleveland Plain Dealer* add further nuances to the story which neither the comic book nor a tape of the show can reveal. The show finally is not an objective grounding event outside of any telling of it but rather a nexus around which the various narratives revolve. There can be no outside "reality check" for Pekar's stories; they either convince as does an anecdote told by a friend or fail to convince at all.

Pekar's appearances on national television highlight the two halves of his public persona: the feisty file clerk and the autodidact "working-class intellectual" writer. Pekar considers the relations between these elements of his identity in "Hypothetical Quandary."[47] An unnamed Pekar-figure drives to the bakery on Sunday morning; as he goes, he thinks about a call from a representative of a "big publisher" who never got back to him. The call leads him to speculate on what his life would be like if he were to become successful as a writer. He thinks of the leisure and freedom from routine a writer's life would give him, then he considers the consequences:

> But then I'd sort of be out of the struggle, sort of in an ivory tower watching the mainstream of life go by rather than participating in it....
>
> I'd be alienated but I wouldn't think I had the right to feel bad about it. I mean, I'd be a well-paid, famous author. What right would I have to complain about anything?
>
> Maybe my writing would suffer. I've got a pretty unique viewpoint.... I'm a writer but in a lotta ways I've got a working man's outlook on life. I'd have to as long as I've worked at regular day jobs.

As he goes into the bakery, buys some loaves of bread, and walks back to his car, he worries that success might make his life and attitudes more bland and boring. Then he thinks, "But then, knowin' myself, I could always find something to get shook up over and write about. Let's face it, I'm not gonna become a mellow man over night, no matter what happens!" He decides that, since the woman from the publisher didn't call him back, the question of his corruption by success is moot. The story ends as he leans over the bag from the bakery, sniffs deeply, and thinks, "Ah, fresh bread!" His sensual enjoyment of present experience contrasts with his fretful speculations about his career; the "real life" he values so deeply finally stands as his bulwark against cooptation by the high culture to which he aspires as a writer and which he also fears as a threat to his autonomy. His status as a working man gives his writings the authenticity of an eyewitness, just as his role as a writer allows him to separate himself from those who are doomed to a lifetime of workaday drudgery.

"Hypothetical Quandary" raises the question that lies behind *American Splendor* as a cultural product. Why should anyone be interested in the daily life of a hospital file clerk in Cleveland? Pekar must tread the thin line in documentary realism between an accurate, compelling rendering of experience and the too precise recreation of boredom. He casts himself as an American lower-class Everyman, while his idiosyncratic personality and quirky perspective on life raise his stories and vignettes beyond the banality of a camera eye; he is at once both universal and unique.

American Splendor is finally not precisely an autobiographical project but more of a "Life and Times." Pekar's works look two ways: the stories featuring the Pekar figure are introspective and revelatory like confessions and autobiographies, and the short tales and vignettes look outside the self of Harvey Pekar to examine, celebrate, and decry the customs and mores of contemporary American society. But these are not two separate categories; the pieces without Pekar finally show as much about the observer as the observed, while Pekar's stories of his personal triumphs and tragedies form an extended critique of a cultural situation which is finally hostile to the assertion of individuality.

The tension between the public demands of society and the private impulses of individuals is the subject of several stories in *American Splendor*'s twelve-year run, but "society" is rarely the organized apparatus of the state as much as it is the attitudes and actions of other individuals. One place where Pekar does butt heads with social institutions is in "Jury Duty,"[48] where Harvey refuses to participate in what he perceives to be an unjust legal system, to the chagrin of the prosecutor, the amusement of the defense attorney, and the bafflement of the judge.

A more typical example of the way public concerns become private ones is "May 4–5, 1970," drawn by Brian Bram (figure 22),[49] which deals with the personal consequences of the National Guard shootings at Kent State University. The splash panel sets the scene in two phases of historical time. The panel consists of newspaper clippings laid on top of one another; their headlines show how history moves from the other side of the globe to become a local concern though still a public one: "Sihanouk Ousted"; "Nixon Orders Troops into Cambodia"; "Nat'l Guard Fires on Students at Kent

Figure 22. Harvey Pekar and Brian Bram, "May 4–5, 1970," page 1
© Harvey Pekar

State." Paper-clipped to the clippings are notes bearing the dates of their publication, showing that we see these events in retrospect. The scalloped lines around the title dates foreshadow the tensions which arise in the story, and the dates themselves suggest that the story will be about the consequences of the action at Kent State, since the killings happened on May 4, the newspaper tells us, and the story covers May 4–5.

In the story the Pekar figure, here called Carl Alesci, chats with a middle-aged plasterer named Mr. Lucarelli at the hospital where they both work. When the talk turns to the recent troubles at nearby Kent State, the two men find that they disagree about the students' right to protest. Carl maintains that the students are peaceful, while Lucarelli becomes indignant, and says, "They keep on raisin' hell, the police need to *shoot* a couple of 'em!" Carl breaks off the conversation. The next day, after the shootings by the National Guard, Carl is asked to wear a black armband with a peace symbol on it to protest the killings; after some hesitation, he accepts. Lucarelli spots Carl with the armband and confronts him about it, and the two men argue sharply.

Later that day, Carl, appalled at the older man's insensitivity and at his hypocrisy of touting law and order while remaining friends with a local mobster, snubs Lucarelli in the cafeteria and in the hallway. After work in the parking lot, Lucarelli tries to make up with Carl, who fiercely demands that the older man admit that he has the right to his own opinion. The story ends with Lucarelli gazing sadly as the still angry Carl stomps away; the last panel is an iconographic image of the "generation gap."

Here history is a chain of events that leads inexorably from Cambodia to a hospital parking lot half a world away, and the split between public history and private autobiography becomes an illusory one. The headlines at the story's beginning link up with the protests at the local college, pass to Carl through his brother-in-law, "He lives in Kent, y'know," and through the newspapers, to spark this conflict between friends; the history of the newspaper headlines is acted out in miniature between the two men. Attitudes like Lucarelli's, the story implies, bring about the killings at Kent State; reactions like Carl's are what end the war in Vietnam. There are no heroes or villains in this story, just people acting in their daily lives.

Carl is not passionately antiwar; he is initially puzzled about how to react to the student protests, and he hesitates before accepting the armband because, "I might get some people here mad at me."

His confrontation with Lucarelli is a result not of his political convictions but of his personal, almost instinctive revulsion to the shooting of the students. While the story has little sympathy with Lucarelli's political views, they are explained at least partly by his immigrant's loyalty to his new country; he says fiercely, "Ay, I don't consider myself Italian—I'm an American!!!" Carl's rejection of his friendly overtures at the end is morally ambiguous; the story shows Carl to be right in his views but self-righteous and hurtful in his actions.

Pekar himself emphasizes the negative aspects of the persona's behavior. He compared this story to another one in which he treats lower-class political attitudes, and he told an interviewer, "In both, I show myself taking a self-righteous attitude toward older people who have hard-line right-wing political positions. In the Kent State story I am actually *mean* to an old plasterer after he tries to bring about a reconciliation."[50] In this story, the Kent State killings are important not solely as an event in a public political process but because they lead people to act badly toward one another.

While Pekar's relentless examination of his private concerns might seem to be a shrinking away from the kind of historical issues that Jack Jackson and Art Spiegelman confront directly, all three really have much in common. Jackson does deal with sweeping historical processes involving complex cultural interactions, but *Comanche Moon* and *Los Tejanos* depict history through the eyes of individual characters such Quanah Parker and Juan Seguin. In the single person of Quanah Parker we can read the fates of both the white race and the red; in Juan Seguin we see a place where cultures momentarily came together, only to split apart again. In *Maus,* Art Spiegelman takes on an even more problematic historical event, the Holocaust, but he uses the personal relation between Vladek and Art as the fulcrum to move his ambitious project.

Individuals are the means by which larger units of history become accessible and explicable; Vladek Spiegelman enables us to see the piles of bodies in the death camp that we would otherwise be unable to look at, because we know that Vladek might well have been one of those bodies, but was not. Harvey Pekar's *American Splendor* takes this emphasis on the individual even further and in so doing explodes the distinction between public and private history. The large movements of nations and institutions that we call history finally become an aggregate of individual choices and actions, and Harvey Pekar's refusal to serve on a jury may ultimately be as significant in its own way as a Supreme Court decision. Harvey Pekar's insistence on the importance of daily life finally is not self-aggrandizement or solipsism but rather an evocation of the inescapable interconnections between human beings.

Why history, personal or otherwise, in comic-book form? Comic books have traditionally staked their appeal to readers on their mythopoeic and imaginative power, not on a connection to literal truth. While the verbal/visual dialectic of sequential art lends itself to a variety of narrative effects which can communicate a great deal of complex information (such as names, dates, chronology, and so forth) while also rendering specific incidents with an immediate and visceral impact, comic books have generally emphasized the physical side of the dialectic and have tended to show grandiose violations of the laws of physics in the context of the most basic sort of Manichean, good-versus-evil conflicts. The underground comix forever demonstrated that the fantasy and escapism of comic books was an artificially imposed cultural constraint, but the willfully adversarial and transgressive stance of the comix ensured that they would remain at the fringes of the culture at large.

The disappearance of a coherent underground movement in the late 1970s left behind a number of inventive and ambitious creators who were convinced of the power of the sequential art medium and were steeped in its peculiar techniques, such as Jack Jackson and Art Spiegelman, as well as newcomers to the field who had been energized by the accomplishments of the comix but were interested in writing other kinds of stories, as was Harvey Pekar. In addition, the undergrounds introduced the potential of the medium to an audience of readers who either had been unfamiliar with comics in general or had associated them solely with juvenile literature.

The move to history in comic-book form is an implicit rejection of the death grip that fantasy has long held on the medium. At the same time, as modern culture becomes less print oriented and more visually literate, comic books become more attractive as a narrative form. Comics are much less linear than prose and more simultaneous in the narrative effects that are possible, while they remain connected to traditional prose narratives by their extensive generic and thematic heritage.

The works of Jack Jackson, Art Spiegelman, and Harvey Pekar hardly constitute a coherent "movement" in contemporary comics. Many artists continue to work in the by now familiar underground modes, and others have transformed the superhero and adventure genres into vehicles for "adult" narratives.[51] Other developments ·in the comic-book scene, like the emergence of self-published "new-ave" comics and various other "alternative" productions, may have far-reaching effects on the cultural place of comic books. But when comic books become an appropriate medium for new visions of American history, for startling examinations of epochal events such as the Holocaust, and for bluntly honest depictions of the individual's plight in modern society, and when these productions vie for literary awards with biographies of Chaucer, then certainly the realm of Superman and Mighty Mouse has undergone a revolution. Pekar fiercely states the conviction implicit in the works of creators such as Jack Jackson and Art Spiegelman:

> Comics is as wide an area as prose. It's a medium, and it can be used for fiction, for non-fiction, for any number of purposes. And the fact that it's been used in such a limited way is totally crazy. It's some kind of historical aberration, I think. What I hope people start to realize is that comics can be as versatile as any other medium. . . . What it takes [for comics to gain a wider audience] is for people to realize that comics aren't an intrinsically limited form. When more people do that, and when more good work is produced, [it will happen]. Because nothing will attract people to comics like good work. If people have a prejudice against them, nothing will negate that prejudice like good work.[52]

In his first appearance on David Letterman's television talk show, Harvey Pekar gave a succinct and heartfelt explanation of why he works in the comic-book form. He said, "It's words and pictures. And you can do anything you want with words and pictures." As the sequential art medium begins to cast off the long decades of critical scorn and cultural marginalization, more and more creators are discovering that what they want to do with words and pictures is to tell true stories.

1. The phrase appears as a subtitle to two collections of selections from Pekar's comic books: *From Off the Streets of Cleveland Comes—American Splendor: The Life and Times of Harvey Pekar* (New York: Doubleday, 1986); and *From Off the Streets of Cleveland Comes—More American Splendor: The Life and Times of Harvey Pekar* (New York: Doubleday, 1987).

2. Robert Crumb, introduction to *American Splendor: The Life and Times of Harvey Pekar*.

3. Harvey Pekar, "Stories about Honesty, Money, and Misogyny," interview with Gary Groth (August 1984), *Comics Journal* 97 (April 1985):46.

4. Robert Crumb, *American Splendor: The Life and Times of Harvey Pekar*, introduction.

5. Harvey Pekar, interview, tape recording, Cleveland, Ohio, 11 November 1988.

6. Donald M. Fiene, "From Off the Streets of Cleveland: The Life and Work of Harvey Pekar," *Comics Journal* 97 (April 1985):73.

7. Harvey Pekar and Robert Crumb, "A Fantasy," *American Splendor* no. 1 (1976).

8. Harvey Pekar, Greg Budgett, and Gary Dumm, "Awaking to the Terror of the New Day," *American Splendor* no. 3 (1978).

9. Budgett's work does not appear in *American Splendor* nos. 9 and 10.

10. Fiene, "Life and Work of Harvey Pekar," 69–70.

11. Harvey Pekar, "Stories about Honesty," 49.

12. Writers of autobiographical stories in the comix include, among others, Aline Kominsky-Crumb, Guy Colwell, Dori Seda, Spain Rodriguez, and, as I will note below, Robert Crumb. More recently, artists such as Lynda Barry and Michael Doogan have produced autobiographical stories in comics form.

13. Harvey Pekar, interview, 11 November 1988.

14. Justin Green, *Binky Brown Meets the Holy Virgin Mary* (Berkeley: Last Gasp Eco-Funnies, 1972).

15. Pekar's comic book stories appeared in *The People's Comics* (1972), *Bizarre Sex* no. 4 (1975), *Comix Book* no. 4 (1976), *Snarf* no. 6 (1976), and *Flamed Out Funnies* no. 1 (1976). Pekar tells the story of his friendship with Crumb in "The Young Crumb Story," *American Splendor* no. 4 (1979), and "A Fantasy," *American Splendor* no. 1 (1976).

16. Robert Crumb, *Big Ass Comics* no. 2 (San Francisco: Rip Off Press, 1971).

17. *Tales from the Leather Nun* (Berkeley: Last Gasp Eco-Funnies, 1973).

18. *Zap* no. 10 (Berkeley: Print Mint, 1982).

19. Both from *The People's Comics* (Princeton, Wisc.: Kitchen Sink Press, 1972).

20. Robert Crumb, "The Confessions of R. Crumb" (1972).

21. Some of Crumb's recent autobiographical stories, like "Uncle Bob's Mid-Life Crisis," *Weirdo* 7 (Berkeley: Last Gasp Eco-Funnies, 1983), seem to be influenced by Pekar's more mundane approach, but as one critic notes, "despite his serious theme, Crumb still plays his tormented self-pity mainly for laughs." Steve Monaco, "A Worthwhile (But Weird) Grab-bag," review of *Weirdo*, *Comics Journal* 106 (March 1986):31.

22. Harvey Pekar and Kevin Brown, "Grubstreet, U.S.A.," *American Splendor* no. 8 (1983).

23. Ibid.

24. Harvey Pekar and Gary Dumm, "Katherine Mansfield," *American Splendor* no. 9 (1984), rear cover.

25. Harvey Pekar, "Stories about Honesty," 46.

26. Harvey Pekar, interview, 11 November 1988.

27. Harvey Pekar and Spain Rodriguez, "A Case Quarter," *American Splendor* no. 11 (1986), inside front cover.

28. Harvey Pekar and Robert Crumb, "The Last Supper," *American Splendor* no. 8 (1983), inside front cover.

29. Harvey Pekar, interview, 11 November 1988.

30. Harvey Pekar, Joyce Brabner, and Val Mayerik, "A Marriage Album," *American Splendor* no. 10 (1985).

31. Harvey Pekar, interview, 11 November 1988.

32. Harvey Pekar and Gary Dumm, "Overheard in the Cleveland Public Library," *American Splendor* no. 3 (1978).

33. Harvey Pekar and Michael T. Gilbert, "Library Story: Take Two," *American Splendor* no. 4 (1979), inside rear cover.

34. Harvey Pekar, interview. 11 November 1988.

35. Harvey Pekar and Val Mayerik, "A Harvey Pekar Story," *American Splendor* no. 9 (1984).

36. Harvey Pekar and Frank Stack, "Jack Dickens' Comic Kingdom," *American Splendor* no. 12 (1987).

37. Harvey Pekar and Val Mayerik, "At the Bindery," ibid.

38. Harvey Pekar and Robert Crumb, *American Splendor* no. 5 (1980), front cover.

39. Harvey Pekar, Val Mayerik, and James Sherman, "Hysteria," *American Splendor* no. 12 (1986).

40. Harvey Pekar and Gerry Shamray, "An Everyday Horror Story," *American Splendor* no. 5 (1980).

41. Harvey Pekar and Gerry Shamray, "Late Night with David Letterman," *American Splendor* no. 12 (1987).

42. Pekar's short career as a media celebrity apparently ended with his 31 August 1988 appearance on the Letterman show. Increasingly impatient with what he saw as Letterman's condescension and triviality, and resolved to "go out with a bang," Pekar badgered Letterman about the legal problems of General Electric, NBC's parent corporation. Letterman tried to quell Pekar and the show dissolved into rowdy bickering. Pekar explains his actions and motivations concerning his television appearances in Harvey Pekar, "Me 'n' Dave Letterman," *Cleveland Plain Dealer*, 1 February 1987, p. 1 (H); Harvey Pekar, "Late Night of the Soul with David Letterman," *Village Voice*, 25 August 1987, pp. 45–46; Harvey Pekar, "Getting Dave's Goat," *Cleveland Edition*, September 22, 1988, pp. 1+; and Harvey Pekar, Joe Zabel, and Gary Dumm, "My Struggle with Corporate Corruption and Network Philistinism," *American Splendor* no. 13 (1988). Another analysis of the controversial show is given in James Hynes, "The Big Shill?" *In These Times* (21–27 September 1988):24+.

43. Pekar gives further background to his appearance on this show in "Me 'n' Dave Letterman."

44. Pekar, "Late Night of the Soul," 45.

45. Harvey's words in the story are a nearly exact quotation of the opening paragraph of a recent article by Pekar, "The Potential of Comics," *Comics Journal* 123 (July 1988):81–88.

46. Pekar might have been hesitant in his answer because he felt that he was losing the attention of the audience, of whom he said, "If you used words longer than two syllables, or talked about anything halfway serious, you could feel them going to sleep." Pekar, "Me 'n' Dave Letterman," p. 4 (H).

47. Harvey Pekar and Robert Crumb, "Hypothetical Quandary," *American Splendor* no. 9 (1984).

48. Harvey Pekar and Sue Cavey, "Jury Duty," *American Splendor* no. 9 (1983).

49. Harvey Pekar and Brian Bram, "May 4–5, 1970," *American Splendor* no. 2 (1977).

50. Pekar, "Stories about Honesty," 50. Note Pekar's total equation of the actions of the persona with his own personal behavior.

51. See Lloyd Rose, "Comic Books for Grown-Ups," *Atlantic*, August 1986, pp. 77–80.

52. Harvey Pekar, interview, 11 November 1988.

Bibliography

Abbott, Lawrence L. "Comic Art: Characteristics and Potentialities of a Narrative Medium." *Journal of Popular Culture* 19 (Spring 1986): 155–173.

Aldridge, Alan, and George Perry. *Penguin Book of Comics.* Harmondsworth, England: Penguin Books, 1967.

Becker, Stephen. *Comic Art in America.* New York: Simon and Schuster, 1949.

Brown, Dee. *Bury My Heart at Wounded Knee.* New York: Holt, Rinehart and Winston, 1970.

Carroll, John M. Introduction. *The Sand Creek Massacre: A Documentary History.* New York: Sol Lewis, 1973.

Daniels, Les. *Comix: A History of Comic Books in America.* New York: Bonanza Books, 1971.

Drinnon, Richard. *Facing West: The Metaphysics of Indian-Hating and Empire-Building.* New York: Minneapolis: University of Minnesota Press, 1980.

Eisner, Will. *Comics and Sequential Art.* Tamarac, Fla.: Poorhouse Press, 1985.

Estren, Mark James. *A History of Underground Comics.* San Francisco: Straight Arrow, 1974.

Feiffer, Jules. *The Great Comic Book Heroes.* New York: Dial Press, 1965.

Fiene, Donald. "From Off the Streets of Cleveland: The Life and Work of Harvey Pekar." *Comics Journal* no. 97 (April 1985): 65–84.

———, comp. "Pekar Index." *Comics Journal* no. 97 (April 1985): 86–88.

Fiore, R. "Funnybook Roulette." *Comics Journal* no. 118 (December 1987): 43–46.

Fischel, Jack, and Sanford Pinsker, eds. *Literature, the Arts, and the Holocaust.* Holocaust Studies Annual, vol. 3. Greenwood, Fla.: Penkevill Publishing, 1987.

Foote, Shelby. *The Civil War: A Narrative.* 2 vols. New York: Random House, 1958.

Gaines, William M. Interview by Dwight Decker and Gary Groth. *Comics Journal* no. 81 (May 1983): 53–84.

Gates, David. "The Light Side of Darkness." *Newsweek* (22 September 1986): 79.

Gehr, Richard. Review of *Maus: A Survivor's Tale,* by Art Spiegelman. *Artforum* (February 1987): 10–11.

Gopnik, Adam. "Comics and Catastrophe." *New Republic,* 22 June 1987, pp. 29–34.

Goulart, Ron. *Great History of Comic Books.* Chicago: Contemporary Books, 1986.

Greeley, Horace. *The American Conflict.* 2 vols. Hartford: O.D. Case, 1864–1867.

Grossman, Robert. "Mauschwitz." *Nation,* 10 January 1987, pp. 23–24.

Hamilton, William. "Revelation Rays and Pain Stars." *New York Times Book Review,* 7 December 1986, p. 71.

Highsmith, Doug. "Comic Books: A Guide to Information Sources." *RQ* 27 (Winter 1987): 202–209.

Holtsmark, Erling B. "*Magnus Robot-Fighter:* The Future Looks at the Present through the Past." *Journal of Popular Culture* 12 (1979):702−720.

Horn, Maurice. *Comics of the American West.* New York: Winchester Press, 1977.

——, ed. *The World Encyclopedia of Comics.* New York: Chelsea House, 1976.

Inge, M. Thomas. *Handbook of American Popular Literature.* New York: Greenwood Press, 1988.

Jackson, Jack. *Comanche Moon.* San Francisco: Rip Off Press/Last Gasp, 1979.

——. "Tejano Cartoonist." Interview with Bill Sherman (28 August 1981). *Comics Journal* no. 61 (Winter 1981):100−111.

——. "Jack Jackson on His Work in the Underground and His New Book, *Los Tejanos.*" Interview with Gary Groth (10 June 1982). *Comics Journal* no. 75 (September 1982):75−84.

——. *Los Tejanos.* Stamford: Conn.: Fantagraphics Books, 1982.

——. "Jaxon." Interview by Bruce Sweeney. *Comics Interview* no. 9 (March 1984): 40−49.

——. Interview with Gary Groth. *Comics Journal* no. 100 (July 1985):111−114.

——. "Learning Texas History: The Painless Way." *Comics Journal* no. 119 (January 1988):97−100.

Johnson, Robert Underwood, and Clarence Clough Buel, eds. *Battles and Leaders of the Civil War.* 4 vols. New York: Century, 1884−1888.

Kennedy, Jay, ed. *The Official Underground and Newave Comix Price Guide.* Cambridge, Mass.: Boatner Norton, 1982.

Kurtzman, Harvey. Interview by Kim Thompson and Gary Groth (Spring 1981). *Comics Journal* no. 67 (October 1981):68−99.

Legman, Gershon. *Love and Death: A Study in Censorship.* New York: Breaking Point, 1949.

Lupoff, Dick, and Don Thompson, eds. *All in Color for a Dime.* New Rochelle, N.Y.: Arlington House, 1970.

Monaco, Steve. "A Worthwhile (But Weird) Grab-bag." Review of *Weirdo. Comics Journal* no. 106 (March 1986):31.

Overstreet, Robert M. *Official Overstreet Comic Book Price Guide.* Cleveland, Tenn.: Overstreet Publications, annual.

Pekar, Harvey. "Stories about Honesty, Money, and Misogyny." Interview with Gary Groth (August 1984). *Comics Journal* no. 97 (April 1985):44−64.

——. *From Off the Streets of Cleveland Comes . . . American Splendor: The Life and Times of Harvey Pekar.* New York: Doubleday, 1986.

——. "*Maus* and Other Topics." *Comics Journal* no. 113 (December 1986):54−57.

——. *From Off the Streets of Cleveland Comes . . . More American Splendor: The Life and Times of Harvey Pekar.* New York: Doubleday, 1987.

——. "Late Night of the Soul with David Letterman." *Village Voice,* 25 August 1987, pp. 45−46.

——. "Me 'n' Dave Letterman." *Cleveland Plain Dealer,* 1 February 1987, p. 1 (H).

——. "Getting Dave's Goat." *Cleveland Edition,* September 22, 1988, p. 1+.

——. "The Potential of Comics." *Comics Journal* no. 123 (July 1988):81−88.

Phelps, Donald. "Word and Image." *Comics Journal* no. 97 (April 1985):41−43.

Prucha, Francis P. *American Indian Policy in Crisis.* Norman: University of Oklahoma Press, 1976.

Reitberger, Reinhold, and Wolfgang Fuchs. *Comics: Anatomy of a Mass Medium.* Boston: Little, Brown, 1972.

Robinson, Jerry. *The Comics: An Illustrated History of Comic Strip Art.* New York: G. P. Putnam's Sons, 1974.

Rose, Lloyd. "Comic Books for Grown-Ups." *Atlantic,* August 1986, pp. 77−80.

Rosenfeld, Alvin. "The Problematics of Holocaust Literature." In *Confronting the Ho-*

locaust: The Impact of Elie Wiesel, ed. Alvin H. Rosenfeld and Irving Greenberg. Bloomington: Indiana University Press, 1978.

Sawyer, Michael. "Albert Lewis Kanter and the Classics: The Man behind the Gilberton Company." *Journal of Popular Culture* 20 (1987): 1–18.

Shelton, Gilbert, Fred Todd, and Don Baumgart. "Rip Off Press: The Publishing Company That's a Little like the Weather." Interview by Diana Schutz. *Comics Journal* no. 92 (August 1984): 69–83.

Sheridan, Martin. *The Comics and Their Creators.* Boston: Hale, Cushman and Flint, 1942.

Slotkin, Richard. *Regeneration through Violence: The Mythology of the American Frontier, 1600–1860.* Middletown, Conn.: Wesleyan University Press, 1973.

———. *The Fatal Environment: The Myth of the Frontier in the Age of Industrialization, 1800–1890.* Middletown, Conn.: Wesleyan University Press, 1985.

Spiegelman, Art. *Maus: A Survivor's Tale.* New York: Pantheon Books, 1986.

Spiegelman, Art, and Françoise Mouly. "Jewish Mice, Bubblegum Cards, Comics Art, and Raw Possibilities." Interview by Joey Cavalieri (New York, 1980–1981). *Comics Journal* no. 65 (August 1981): 98–125.

Steranko, James. *The Steranko History of Comics.* 2 vols. Wyomissing, Pa.: Supergraphics, 1970–1972.

Thompson, Don, and Dick Lupoff, eds. *The Comic-Book Book.* New Rochelle, N.Y.: Arlington House, 1973.

Tucker, Ken. "Cats, Mice, and History—The Avant-Garde of the Comic Strip." *New York Times Book Review,* 26 May 1985, p. 3.

Waugh, Coulton. *The Comics.* New York: Macmillan, 1947.

Wertham, Fredric. *Seduction of the Innocent.* New York: Holt, Rinehart and Winston, 1954. Reprint. Port Washington, N.Y.: Kennikat Press, 1972.

Weschler, Lawrence. "Mighty 'Maus.'" *Rolling Stone,* 20 November 1986, p. 103.

Index

Adorno, T. W., 97
Air Pirates Funnies, 110
Anderson, Major Robert: commander of Fort Sumter, 17–19, 37; in prose passage, 18–19, 30; in "April, 1861: Fort Sumter," 24–26, 32–33, 43
Animal comic books, 4, 97, 103; as genre, 109–12; in underground comix, 110–11; by R. Crumb, 111. *See also* Spiegelman, Art, *Maus*
Anthony, Major Scott J., 66
"April, 1861: Fort Sumter": discussed, 20–36, 88; compared with prose passage, 20, 22, 24–26 *passim*, 29–32, 33–35, 43; panel breakdowns in, 22; compared with "First Shot," 37, 39–44 *passim*; compared with *Los Tejanos*, 88
Archie comics, 13, 49

Barks, Carl, 10; use of animal characters, 109
Batman, 7, 10, 13, 36
Beauregard, General Pierre G. T.: Confederate commander at Fort Sumter siege, in prose passage, 17–18, 19; in *Classics Illustrated* excerpt, 25, 43
Bent, Robert, 67–68
Blake, William, 6
Brabner, Joyce, 137, 139
Bradbury, Ray, 39
Bram, Brian, 149
Breakdowns: defined, 20–22; by Jack Kirby, 26, 33, 43; in sequential art, 34; by Harvey Kurtzman, 40; by Jack Jackson, 72; by Art Spiegelman, 104; in *American Splendor*, 127

Brown, Dee: *Bury My Heart at Wounded Knee*, 67–68
Budgett, Greg, 126–27

Captain America, 28
Cavey, Sue, 139
Chivington, Colonel John M., 65–70, 73–74
Classics Illustrated comic books: described, 14; audience for, 14, 35–36; excerpt from discussed, 15, 16, 17, 20–36; cultural role of, 31–32, 92, 93; narrative strategies of, 34–35, 82; renamed from *Classics Comics*, 35–36; compared to Jackson's works, 61. *See also* Gilberton Company
Comanches (American Indians), 61, 75, 92. *See also* Jackson, Jack, *Comanche Moon*
Comic books: as literature, 3, 5, 10–11, 36, 50, 93, 97, 154; distinct from comic strips, 6–9; cultural hostility towards, 7, 15, 32, 35, 44, 97. *See also* Sequential art
Comic strips: distinct from comic books, 6–9; humor strips, 6–7, 133, 135, 137; continuity strips, 6–9
Comics Code Authority: censors comic books, 7, 15, 44–45; described, 48
Comics Code: described, 48–49; influence on comic books, 7, 48–50; and underground comix, 50–54, 72, 74; revision of, 51; parodied, 51; mentioned, 79. *See also* Comics Code Authority
Crumb, Robert: collaboration with Pekar, 52, 122, 129, 130, 135, 137, 139, 148–49; work in underground comix,

Kelly, Walt: *Pogo*, 10; as animal comic, 109

Kirby, Jack: his art discussed, 20–36; page layouts, 20, 23–24, 26, 28; style of, 28, 35; art compared with "First Shot," 37, 39, 41

Korean War: in war comics, 40; affects comics sales, 42

Kurtzman, Harvey: edits war comics, 15, 36–37, 61; his Nagasaki story, 39; on war technology, 42; narrative strategies, 42–43, 44, 79; influence on underground comix, 45; compared with Jackson, 64–65; his "Custer's Last Stand," 83; as history writer, 93, 117. *See also* "First Shot"

Legman, Gershon, 9–10

Letterman, David, 143, 144, 146–48, 154

Mad magazine: survives Comics Code, 15, 46, 50; Kurtzman editor of, 46; and underground comix, 45, 53

Manson, Charles, 53

Mayerik, Val, 139

McCay, Winsor: *Little Nemo in Slumberland*, 8

Mesmer, Otto: *Felix the Cat*, 109

Mickey Mouse: comic strip, 8; as animal comic, 109, 110

Mouly, Françoise: quoted, 104; as character in *Maus*, 112–14, 116

Nagasaki: E.C. story of, 39

Orwell, George: *Animal Farm*, 110

Osborne, Jim, 52

Parker, Quanah: biography discussed, 75–84; mentioned, 61, 85, 92, 152. *See also* Jack Jackson, *Comanche Moon*

Patton, Jack: see *Texas History Movies*

Pekar, Harvey: autobiography, 4, 11, 121–23, 133, 137, 148–49; and underground comix, 52, 128–29, 153; narrative strategies of, 123, 142; as observer, 123; themes, 127; and literary realism, 132–33; stories collected, 143; works by: *American Splendor*, 3, 4, 10, 52; described, 121–22; "Awaking to the Terror of the New

Day," 123–28; "Awaking to the Terror of the Same Old Day," 126; "American Splendor Assaults the Media," 129–31, 144; "Grubstreet, U.S.A.," 132; "Katherine Mansfield," 132–33; "A Case Quarter," 135; "A Marriage Album," 137–39; "Overheard in the Cleveland Public Library," 139–42; "Library Story: Take Two," 139–42; "A Harvey Pekar Story," 142–43; "Hysteria," 144; "An Everyday Horror Story," 144; "Late Night with David Letterman," 144–46; "Hypothetical Quandary," 148–49; "Jury Duty," 149; "May 4–5, 1970," 149–52

Pryor, Roger, 18–19, 30

Raymond, Alex: *Flash Gordon*, 8

Rifas, Leonard, 56

Rosenfield, John, Jr. *See Texas History Movies*

Rowlandson, Thomas, 6

Ruffin, Edmund, 18, 19, 20, 29, 37

Sand Creek Massacre: history of, 62; in "'Nits Make Lice,'" 62–74, 75

Segar, E. C.: *Popeye* (*Thimble Theater*), 8

Seguin, Juan N.: biography of, 85–93 *passim*; mentioned, 61, 152. *See also Los Tejanos*

Sequential art: defined, 5–6; visual subtext in, 20, 26–28, 32–33, 39, 43; compared with prose, 20, 26, 34, 43, 67–68, 74; reading of, 22, 34, 44; textual spaces in, 22, 26, 34–35, 37, 79; flashbacks in, 25, 43; verbal elements in, 22–23, 33, 37, 87–88; word balloons in, 22–23, 34–35, 37, 44; analogies to other media, 28, 34, 147–48; sound effects in, 34, 37, 40, 79; voyeurism in, 72; as process analysis, 115. *See also* comic books; comic strips

Shamray, Gerry, 139, 146

Skull Comix, 54–56

Slow Death Comix, 54–56

Spain (pseud. Spain Rodriguez), 133–35

Spiegelman, Art: National Book Critics Circle Award nomination, 4, 5, 96, 98, 154; work in underground comix, 52, 96, 98; editor of *Raw*, 96, 121; use of animal characters, 96, 100, 102–07,

Spiegelman, Art (*continued*)
109–13; drawing style, 100, 103–06;
narrative strategies, 102, 114; works
compared with Pekar, 122, 152; works
by: *Maus*, 3, 4, 5, 10, 11, 52, 96–118;
as atrocity story, 74; as autobiography,
98–101, 115–16; "Prisoner of the
Hell Planet," 98–100; "Maus" (first
version), 103–06 *passim*; as animal
comic, 109–14, 115
Stout, William: work in underground
comix, 56; his cover art, 71
Superman, 7, 13, 122, 152

Tejanos (Texas-Mexicans), 4, 60, 61,
85–87, 88–93. *See also* Jackson, Jack,
Los Tejanos
Texas History Movies, 79, 92
Tom and Jerry, 110
True adventure comic books, 14
True Comics, 14
Two-Fisted Tales, 15, 40, 42, 45, 93

Uncle Scrooge comic book, 10, 13, 36,
109

Underground comix: mentioned, 4; and
animal comics, 10–11, 110–11; compared with E.C. comics, 45, 53–55,
56; influence of Harvey Kurtzman on,
45; defined, 51; aesthetics of, 52–53,
68, 70, 74, 76–77, 153; and feminism,
53–54, 71–73, 74; as educational
comics, 55–56; and contemporary
adult comics, 62, 67, 75–77, 153, 154;
and autobiography, 118, 128–29
Uncle Scrooge: comic book, 10, 13, 36,
109

Veitch, Tom, 53
Vietnam War: and underground comix,
53, 62; as theme, 70–71

Wagner, Geoffrey, 9–10
Warner Brothers, 109
Wertham, Fredric: attacks comic books,
9–10, 35; *Seduction of the Innocent*,
49; parodied, 51
Wiesel, Eli, 97
Wilson, S. Clay, 52, 53